LEGAL RESEARCH

IN A NUTSHELL®

TWELFTH EDITION

MORRIS L. COHEN
Late Librarian and Emeritus Professor of Law
Yale Law School

KENT C. OLSON
Head of Research Services
University of Virginia Law Library

WEST
ACADEMIC
PUBLISHING

COPYRIGHT © 1968, 1971, 1978, 1985, 1992, 1996 WEST PUBLISHING CO.
© 2000 West Group
© West, a Thomson business, 2003
© 2007 Thomson/West
© 2010 Thomson Reuters
© 2013 LEG, Inc. d/b/a West Academic Publishing
© 2016 LEG, Inc. d/b/a West Academic
   444 Cedar Street, Suite 700
   St. Paul, MN 55101
   1-877-888-1330

West, West Academic Publishing, and West Academic are trademarks of West Publishing Corporation, used under license.

Printed in the United States of America

ISBN: 978-1-63460-462-8

For Etta

PREFACE

This is the twelfth edition of a book that began as the late Morris Cohen's brainchild in the 1960s. Times have certainly changed in those fifty years, but the need for lawyers, paralegals, and scholars to do legal research effectively and confidently remains. It has been my honor to collaborate with Morris and to carry on his work.

Most legal research can be performed from anywhere with an Internet connection, but keyword retrieval and search algorithms have not fully supplanted the sophisticated editorial tools that shaped our legal literature. Many online sources are based on printed works and incorporate their structure and logic, and an understanding of their purpose and scope is needed for effective research whether it is done online or in print. Finding an answer to a legal question is easier than ever. Finding a correct and complete answer requires as much skill as it did in the print era.

This edition of *Legal Research in a Nutshell* omits illustrations of the resources discussed, as small black-and-white screenshots hardly do justice to online resources. Illustrations are instead available on to the *Nutshell*'s companion website (libguides.law.virginia.edu/nutshell12). You are encouraged to view these online illustrations while reading or reviewing each chapter.

The book covers a wide range of government and commercial websites in addition to Westlaw, Lexis, and Bloomberg Law services and print-based resources. The companion website has links to all Internet sites listed and is updated on a regular basis.

Once again I would like to thank my colleagues Kristin Glover and Amy Wharton for their corrections and suggestions on this revision, and for using a draft in their Advanced Legal Research classes. I am also grateful to Amy for her creative and patient work in website design and implementation, and to Carol Sue Wood for helping with the website.

KENT C. OLSON

Charlottesville, Virginia
January 2016

OUTLINE

LEGAL RESEARCH

IN A NUTSHELL®

TWELFTH EDITION

CHAPTER 1

THE RESEARCH PROCESS

Images of some resources discussed in this chapter are at **libguides.law.virginia.edu/nutshell12/ch1**

---

§ 1–1. Introduction

You are about to begin a legal research project, and on your screen there is a blank search box. We all know how to use a search box to find some information, but legal research is much more than that. Legal research is the process of identifying the legal rules that govern an activity and finding sources that explain or analyze those rules. It requires knowing that the information you find is current, accurate and complete. Successful research gives you confidence that you're not missing any important pieces that might undermine the conclusions you reach. You need to learn the many sources of legal information and the ways to access them. This book is devoted to teaching you the topic.

Legal research works hand-in-hand with the legal analysis skills you learn in law school classes like Torts and Constitutional Law. These substantive law school classes teach you to evaluate factual situations and to determine the relevant fields of legal doctrine. Legal research skills give you the ability to identify the specific rules that apply to a particular situation. They lead to the knowledge you need to provide accurate and insightful advice, to draft effective documents, and to defend your clients' rights. Ineffective research wastes time and money, and inaccurate research is malpractice.

§ 1–2.   The Sources of the Law

The law consists of the recorded rules that society will enforce and the procedures by which they are implemented. These rules and procedures are created in various ways, some by elected legislatures and others through judicial decisions. The United States has a federal system, in which each state has its own constitution and its own body of law. The federal and state governments all have three branches—legislative, executive, and judicial—each with lawmaking powers.

As the elected voice of the citizens, the legislature raises and spends money, defines crimes, regulates commerce, and generally determines public policy by enacting statutes. Some of these statutes are broadly worded statements of public policy, while others regulate activity in minute detail.

The executive branch is charged with enforcing the law, and in the process it creates legally binding rules. The president and governors issue executive orders, and administrative agencies make detailed regulations governing activity within their areas of expertise. Agencies also act in a "quasi-judicial" capacity by conducting hearings and issuing decisions to resolve particular disputes. These administrative law sources are less familiar to many people than statutes and court decisions, but they can determine legal rights and responsibilities. Attorneys in heavily regulated areas such as securities law or telecommunications may work more frequently with these agency pronouncements than with statutes or cases.

The judicial branch plays a complex role in this system. Judges apply the language of constitutions and statutes to specific court cases, which often involve circumstances that could not have been foreseen when the laws were enacted. These judicial interpretations can be just as important as the text of the provisions they interpret. The courts have determined, for example, that sexual harassment is a form of employment discrimination under the Civil Rights Act of 1964 even though those words never appear in the statute. Through the power of judicial review, asserted by Chief Justice Marshall in *Marbury v. Madison*, the courts also determine the constitutionality of acts of the legislative and executive branches.

Judges also create and shape the *common law*. In a common law system, the law is expressed in an evolving body of doctrine determined by judges in specific cases, rather than in a group of prescribed abstract principles. The common law grows and changes over time as established rules are tested and adapted to meet new situations.

A core element of the common law is the doctrine of precedent, or *stare decisis* ("let the decision stand"), under which courts are bound to follow earlier decisions. These prior cases provide guidance to courts faced with similar issues, and aid in preventing further disputes. People can study earlier cases, evaluate the legal impact of planned conduct, and modify their behavior to conform to existing rules. Precedent is designed to provide both fairness and stability.

Legal issues are sorted into distinct areas of doctrine such as contract, tort, and property. This provides a framework for analyzing legal situations and applying a particular body of rules. Real life does not always divide neatly into issues of contract or tort, but legal materials generally follow this paradigm. A lawyer with a case involving injury from a defective product, for example, may need to research breach of warranty issues in texts and articles on contracts as well as strict liability and negligence issues in the tort literature.

Other categories that pervade legal thinking include *civil* and *criminal law*, *substance* and *procedure*, and *state* and *federal jurisdiction*. Law students learn how legal issues fit into these frameworks, not only to solve problems but also to know where to look for answers. It is important, however, not to pigeonhole a question too narrowly. Research and analysis within a particular doctrinal area can clarify a specific issue, but most situations contain issues from a number of areas. A lawyer who does thorough research on causation issues but neglects procedural limitations is a lawyer who loses cases.

§ 1-3. The Forms of Legal Information

Effective legal research requires knowledge not only of the legal system, but also of the ways in which legal information is disseminated. Legal literature is comprised of both official, primary statements of the law and an extensive body of unofficial secondary writings. Most information is now accessible online, but some resources are still available only in print. Laws are published chronologically, and researchers need both resources that compile current laws and those that provide access to historical sources.

a. Primary and Secondary Sources

Legal sources differ in the weight they are accorded. Some are binding authority, while others are only persuasive in varying degrees or are useful only as tools for finding other sources. Each source must be used with a sense of its place in the hierarchy of authority.

In evaluating authority, you must distinguish between *primary* and *secondary sources*. Primary sources are the official pronouncements of the government lawmakers: the court decisions, legislation, and regulations that form the basis of the legal doctrine. Not all primary sources have the same force for all purposes. A decision from a state supreme court is *binding* authority in its jurisdiction and must be followed by the lower state courts. A state statute also must be followed within the state. Other primary sources are only *persuasive* authority; a court in one state may be influenced by decisions in other states faced with similar issues, but it is free to make up its own mind.

Works which are not themselves the law, but which discuss or analyze legal doctrine, are considered secondary sources. These include treatises, hornbooks, *Restatements*, and the academic journals known as law reviews. Secondary sources serve a number of important functions in legal research. Scholarly commentaries can clarify the sometimes bewildering array of statutes and court decisions, provide current awareness about developing legal doctrines, and even propose changes in the law. Their footnotes contain extensive references to primary sources and to other secondary material. While they are not the law and are thus never binding authority, secondary sources can be persuasive authority. A judge may be even more influenced by a scholarly article than by decisions from other jurisdictions.

b. Online and Print Resources

Most of the resources used in legal research first appeared in printed form and developed as print publications over several decades or even centuries. Detailed editorial systems such as digests, citators, and annotated codes were created to make sense of the jumble of primary sources.

Lawyers now do more research online than in print, but books are still useful in many situations. Researchers who work solely with an uncontrolled mass of online documents can quickly find themselves drowning in unstructured information. Resources such as treatises and digests, whether used online or in print, continue to provide the invaluable service of organizing material by subject. An online search finds the documents that match your terms, but even a sophisticated search engine may miss important documents with slightly different terminology or issues. Supplementing a keyword search with background reading and subject access may reveal new information, or it can confirm your results and boost your confidence.

Print resources can sometimes be more cost-effective than online searching, and they can make it easier to determine an issue's context. Browsing a table of contents and flipping through related sections can help you see the broader picture and raise issues you might not have considered. The texts, codes, and other print resources that lawyers use are updated regularly to reflect changes. Many have *pocket parts*, supplements that fit inside the back covers of bound volumes, while others are issued in looseleaf binders and updated with supplementary inserts or replacement pages. Try as they might, of course, print resources can never be quite as current as a regularly updated online resource.

Three major online services—Westlaw, Lexis, and Bloomberg Law—are widely used in law schools and in legal practice as comprehensive legal research tools. Law students generally have access to these services through their school's subscriptions, but for other researchers these can be expensive tools. (Much of the information in these services may be available to university faculty and students through Westlaw Campus Research or LexisNexis Academic.)

Many law students tend to limit their research to one or two of the major services, but there is a vast store of documents and information in other resources available from most academic law libraries. Services such as HeinOnline (home. heinonline.org) are designed as repositories of information once accessed only in print, with PDF images of resources such as court reports, statutes, and law journals. Resources such as ProQuest Congressional (congressional.proquest.com) are essential tools in specialized areas. Most law library websites have a directory of online resources to which the library subscribes. Each new resource may require an initial learning curve to understand its features and search syntax, but this is time well spent.

Several online research services provide low-cost access to primary sources. These services generally have thorough coverage of case law and statutes, but they offer a smaller range of secondary sources and other features. Some of these, such as Casemaker (www.casemaker.us) and Fastcase (www.fastcase.com), are offered to lawyers in most jurisdictions as a benefit of state bar membership.

Free Internet sites, particularly those provided by the federal and state governments, can also be valuable sources of legal information. In addition to current statutes and recent case law, government sites also may include once hard-to-find resources such as legislative documents, administrative agency materials, and court documents. The Internet is also an invaluable means of linking scholars and practitioners through websites, blogs, and e-mail.

Google (www.google.com) and other Internet search engines can also help you find relevant sites, although it can be difficult to evaluate results and weed out advertisements and misleading information. Sometimes a web directory will have links to better sites than those that appear at the top of a list of search results. The research guides available from most law school library websites, or directories listing sites by jurisdiction such as Cornell Law School's Legal Information Institute (www.law.cornell.edu), select quality law-related sites. Sites such as these are prepared by experts and have links to sources for cases, statutes, journals, and other materials.

One advantage of major commercial online services over free Internet sites is that their information is generally (but not always) accurate and up to date. Even government sites can present obsolete information without indicating that it is no longer current, and other websites can be biased, selective in coverage, or dangerously out of date. You must always assess the currency and reliability of information, whether found online or in print, before relying on it as an accurate statement of the law.

c. Current and Historical Information

The legal system is created over the course of time, and the law in force today is a combination of old and new enactments and decisions. Older laws generally retain their force and effect until they are expressly repealed or overruled. There are also laws that are just days or weeks old, as legislatures, courts, and executive agencies address issues of current concern. To determine the law that governs a particular situation, you may need access to some sources that are centuries old and others that have just been issued. Even laws no longer in force may be required to interpret documents or resolve disputes.

Lawyers must also keep up with new developments in order to serve their clients. Numerous resources exist to provide current information. New court decisions, statutes, and regulations are readily available on government and commercial websites. Newsletters, looseleaf services, and blogs provide notice and analysis of legal and business developments. In any of the major services, you can set up alerts to notify you of new documents affecting the specific issues you are researching.

Internet resources are increasingly cited in law review articles and court opinions, but online material can be available one day and disappear the next. Hunting around the site or running a site-specific search can often locate material that has been moved, but *link rot* remains a serious problem in legal research. Repositories such as the Internet Archive's Wayback Machine (archive.org/web) provide some access to "obsolete" information, and initiatives such as Perma (perma.cc) offer permanent archives of webpages cited in journal articles and court opinions.

§ 1–4. Legal Language

One of the tasks law students face is mastering a new way of speaking and writing. The law has developed its own means of expression over the centuries. Latin words and phrases are still prevalent, from the familiar writs of *certiorari* and *habeas corpus* to doctrines such as *res ipsa loquitur*, and even everyday words such as *infant* or *issue* may have specialized meanings in legal documents.

You need a good law dictionary to help you understand the language of the law. The leading work, *Black's Law Dictionary* (Bryan A. Garner ed., 10th ed. 2014, also available on Westlaw), provides definitions for more than 50,000 terms, and includes pronunciations and notes on usage. It defines older terms found in historical documents and is updated regularly to explain new legal terminology.

Wolters Kluwer Bouvier Law Dictionary (Stephen Michael Sheppard ed., compact ed. 2011 and desk ed. 2012) has 8,500 entries, far fewer than *Black's*, but its definitions are generally more thorough. The two-volume desk edition includes notes on derivation and usage, with lengthy excerpts from articles and opinions showing how a term is used in legal writing. The paperback compact edition has the same definitions but omits these notes.

Less comprehensive law dictionaries are available for free on the Internet. These include works hosted by FindLaw (dictionary.findlaw.com) and Law.com (dictionary.law.com). Shorter works found in law libraries or bookstores include Steven H. Gifis, *Barron's Law Dictionary* (6th ed. 2010), and Daniel Oran, *Oran's Dictionary of the Law* (4th ed. 2008).

Other language reference works are also available. Bryan A. Garner, editor of *Black's Law Dictionary*, is also author of *Garner's Dictionary of Legal Usage* (3d ed. 2011), which focuses on the way words are used in legal contexts and provides guidance for clear and simple writing. William C. Burton, *Burton's Legal Thesaurus* (5th ed. 2013) can help you identify alternate terms for searching indexes or online databases. Several sources reprint the most memorable uses of legal language. Fred R. Shapiro, *Oxford Dictionary of American Legal Quotations* (1993), the most scholarly of these collections, is arranged by topic with indexes by keyword and author.

§ 1–5.   Legal Citations

Another hurdle in understanding legal literature is decoding the citation form used in most sources. A researcher wishing to read *Tarasoff v. Regents of the University of California*, 551 P.2d 334 (Cal. 1976), needs to know that "551" is the volume number, "334" the page number, and "P.2d" the abbreviation for the *Pacific Reporter, Second Series*, a source for California Supreme Court opinions. This form may seem obscure at first, but in a very succinct manner it provides the information necessary to find the source and to determine its potential value as precedent. All case citations, for example, identify not only where a case can be found but also the issuing court and the year of decision.

The standard guide to legal citation form is *The Bluebook: A Uniform System of Citation* (20th ed. 2015) (www.legalbluebook.com), published by the Harvard Law Review Association. The Bluebook establishes rules both for proper abbreviations and usage of signals such as "cf." and "But see." The Association of Legal Writing Directors' *ALWD Guide to Legal Citation* (5th ed. 2014) is used by some law schools and journals as an alternative to *The Bluebook*. Cornell Law School's Legal Information Institute has an online *Introduction to Basic Legal Citation* (www.law.cornell.edu/citation/), a concise guide that incorporates both *Bluebook* and *ALWD* rules.

Even though most research is done online, *The Bluebook* and other citation systems generally require references to page numbers in printed sources if the material is published in that form. Some online resources have PDF page images that mirror the printed version, while others indicate the printed page numbers in the text of the electronic documents. In some instances, however, a complete citation may still require tracking down the original print publication in the library.

Citations to legal authorities that do not depend on references to particular volume and page numbers are called *public domain* or *medium neutral* citations. Under such a system, official numbers are assigned to documents as they are issued and each paragraph is numbered so that references to specific portions of the text can be identified. This approach has been endorsed by the American Bar Association, and if a public domain citation is available its use is required by *The Bluebook*. Only a few jurisdictions, however, have adopted rules requiring paragraph numbers or other public domain citation features. *Universal Citation Guide* (3d ed. 2014) has guidelines for a uniform public domain format.

No matter what citation rules are followed, part of the puzzle is simply deciphering an abbreviation in order to identify its source. Cases and law review articles contain numerous abbreviations and citations that are cryptic even to experienced researchers. You may be able to retrieve a document by citation from an online service without knowing what the citation means, but that doesn't always work. Reference works such as *Black's Law Dictionary* and *The Bluebook* contain tables listing the major abbreviations found in legal literature, but these are hardly comprehensive. The most convenient guide to abbreviations is probably the free online Cardiff Index to Legal Abbreviations (www.legalabbrevs.cardiff.ac.uk). Mary Miles Prince, *Prince's Bieber Dictionary of Legal Abbreviations* (6th ed. 2009) and Donald Raistrick, *Index to Legal Citations and Abbreviations* (4th ed. 2013) also have broad coverage of both common and obscure abbreviations.

§ 1–6. Online Research Basics

The methods of legal research using specialized resources such as case digests and annotated codes will be discussed in later chapters, but online legal research has several basic characteristics no matter what type of sources are being explored.

The major research services have sought to make research as simple as running an Internet search. You enter your terms in a search box, and the computer presents you with a variety of relevant material sorted by document type (cases, statutes, secondary sources). This can work well, as long as you know what you're looking for and can filter your results quickly to find appropriate documents. If you linger on the initial results page and wander around looking at material that is not particularly helpful in most situations, such as appellate briefs or pending regulations, you will spend your clients' money needlessly. Research is something to approach as a knowledgeable and savvy consumer. It is important not to view online resources like a tourist wandering through a bazaar letting things catch your eye, but like an experienced chef stopping at the store to buy a few essential ingredients for dinner.

Legal research services have millions of documents. Your research projects will require you to cull the limited number of relevant documents from those millions, a professional skill that often requires more than simple Internet-type searches for keywords or phrases. To help you with this, the major legal research services permit much more powerful and focused searches, allowing the use of features such as synonyms, truncation, proximity connectors, and field restrictions for searching specific parts of documents. If you use these search techniques, rather than just rely on a computer program's algorithms and relevancy rankings, you can be confident that you have identified the most important documents.

Which online service to use for a particular research problem (if a choice is available) is a decision based in part on personal preference and in part on the features and resources offered. Law students should learn to use more than one service, if only to be prepared for whatever their employers offer once they enter practice.

This discussion focuses on Westlaw, Lexis, and Bloomberg Law, but remember that lower-cost and free alternatives are available. Preliminary research and straightforward retrieval of documents are tasks particularly well suited to resources that don't incur large expenses for every search or minute spent online. Exploring available resources while in law school will help you understand their strengths and shortcomings once in practice. Features and search approaches vary from site to site, but most sites have help screens or guides to orient new users.

Source Selection. One of the first choices confronting a researcher is whether to search all sources at once, or only in specific sources. Westlaw, Lexis, and Bloomberg Law are all designed so that you can begin with a global search across all sources and then filter your results. It is tempting to begin all your research this way. But if you already know that you need a certain type of document (such as cases or law review articles), it is often more efficient to start by searching in just those sources. You need to know what types of documents you're looking for with either approach; the difference is whether you make that decision before or after your search.

You are also presented with an option of jurisdictions in which to search. You can search all state and federal materials, or you can limit to one or more specific jurisdictions. Whether to limit research to a particular jurisdiction depends on such factors as the purpose of the research and the value of information from other jurisdictions. Sometimes you are interested in information from around the country, but often you need to know the law in one specific jurisdiction.

Searching. Westlaw and Lexis offer two basic methods of searching: plain language, and Boolean terms and connectors. Both services have a single search box in which you enter your query, and they recognize the search method you've chosen. Whichever service you are using, you should understand the strengths of each approach. Bloomberg Law at present recognizes only Boolean searches.

A plain language search allows you to enter a phrase, or a combination of words (e.g., *Is an owner without knowledge of her dog's vicious propensity liable for injuries?* or simply *vicious dog liability knowledge*). The computer assigns relative weights to the terms in a query, depending on how often they appear in the database. It then retrieves the most relevant documents, giving greater weight to the less common terms. Most online keyword searches find only those documents that match their terms, and will never discover related documents that use different terms or involve slightly different facts. Some of the more sophisticated services use algorithms that retrieve some relevant documents with different terms, but relying on algorithms is a poor substitute for exercising your own judgment about the particular facts and issues of your case.

A Boolean search, which can provide greater precision in retrieval, requires learning a structured search syntax. Specific terms or phrases are joined by logical connectors such as *and*, or by proximity connectors indicating the maximum number of words that can separate the search terms (e.g., */10* or *w/10*) or specifying that the words appear in the same sentence (*/s* or *w/sent*) or the same paragraph (*/p* or *w/para*). When used in conjunction with other connectors, an *or* connector in Westlaw (but not in Lexis or Bloomberg Law) is understood between two adjacent search terms. The search *dangerous dog*, for example, looks for documents containing either the word *dangerous* or the word *dog*. To search for a phrase such as "dangerous dog" on Westlaw, you must place the phrase in quotation marks.

Another aspect of Boolean searching is the use of the truncation symbols *!* and * (or *?*, in Lexis). An exclamation point is used to find any word beginning with the specified letters. *Search!*, for example, finds *searcher*, *searched*, and *searching*. Without the truncation symbol, only the word itself and its plural form are retrieved. *Search* retrieves *searches*, but not *searched* or *searching*. The asterisk is less frequently used, but represents a particular character or a limited number of characters. *Legali*e* retrieves either the American *legalize* or the British *legalise*, and *hand*** retrieves *hand*, *handy* or *handle* but not *handgun*.

Why would you want to learn how to construct Boolean searches when you can just enter your terms and get the most relevant documents? There are several reasons. A simple keyword search without connectors may retrieve thousands, or even millions, of documents containing your terms. The most relevant results should appear first, but you may need to filter thousands of documents to make sure you're not missing anything important. A Boolean search puts you in charge, finding only those documents that match your requirements. The number of retrieved documents can be a useful indication of whether your search was appropriate and whether it needs to be broadened or narrowed.

Plain language and Boolean search methods are best suited for different purposes. A plain language search is most useful as a starting point for finding a few highly relevant documents. Because documents are retrieved based on how frequently search terms appear, it is also ideal for finding documents on issues involving frequently used terms such as "summary judgment." Many cases mention the standards for summary judgment, but the few decisions focusing on it in depth would be presented first as most relevant. Boolean searches, which require documents to match a request exactly, are generally more effective when searching for a particular phrase or a precise combination of terms.

If a completed search retrieves a large number of documents, you can narrow your inquiry by using the *Search Within Results* filter on either Westlaw or Lexis. This allows you to search within the retrieved set of documents for specific terms, even if those terms were not included in the initial request. *Search Within Results* accepts only phrases and Boolean connectors; even if you don't use Boolean in your initial search, you may need it to achieve precision.

Advanced Search Screens. Westlaw and Lexis both have advanced search screens, which introduce features that can make your searching much more effective.

On Westlaw, one of these features is a "Term Frequency" tool that allows you to specify that particular terms appear at least a certain number of times in a document. This makes it more likely that retrieved cases or articles will focus on your issues rather than mentioning them in passing. The word *dog* might be used in a saying such as "Every dog has its day," but a search requiring *dog* to appear at least ten times will skip such documents and find those more likely to discuss canine-related issues.

The advanced search screens also give you the opportunity to search within *document fields* (on Westlaw) or *segments* (on Lexis). These are specific parts of a document, such as the title of an article or the name of the judge writing an opinion. Limiting a search to a particular field or segment can produce much more specific results. A search in a case database for *brown* retrieves every decision mentioning a brown dog or a brown truck, but a search in the Title field or Party Name segment for *brown* retrieves only those cases where one of the parties is named Brown.

The list of document fields or segments available on the advanced search screen depends on the particular type of content you've selected to search. An advanced search in all content only lists three fields: Date, Citation, and Name/Title. If you choose to search only cases, however, you have several other fields or segments to choose from. You can easily retrieve a complete list of a judge's opinions by putting her name in the Judge field or Judges segment, or you can combine this request with other search terms to find her opinions on a particular topic. Advanced search screens display sample documents showing what is included in each field.

Bloomberg Law provides some advanced search features, depending on the type of source you select. The court opinions search screen, for example, has fields such as Party Name, Judge, and Date Range.

Results Display. Once you enter a search, the service generally displays a list of results with text excerpts showing where your search terms appear. Results are usually ranked by relevance, but you can opt instead to list the most recent documents first. Your results can be filtered by document type (if you have searched all content) and by other features such as jurisdiction, source, or date, depending on the type of material.

Most documents include *star paging*, which indicates the page breaks in the original printed sources. This allows you to cite to a particular passage in a case, law review article, or other document without having to track down the printed version.

History, Saved Searches, and Alerts. All three services save your previous searches for ninety days or more, allowing you to return to earlier research results and to track your process. They also give you the capability to collect and store documents and searches in folders or workspaces that you can share with colleagues. Perhaps the most powerful of these features is the ability to save a search and have the service automatically run it to check for new material on a daily or weekly basis. This alert feature is a convenient way to stay abreast of developments in a specific case or in an area of interest. Your computer continues to think about an issue, while you move on to other matters.

Citators. Many documents, especially cases, have links not only to the resources they cite, but also to later sources that cite them. This is an invaluable way to find related materials and to bring research forward in time.

If a document has been frequently cited, the services present several ways to focus retrieval to specific types of document or specific treatments. Westlaw and Lexis also let you run searches within the results to see only citing documents that use specific keywords. All three services give you the option to set up a citation alert, which can send you notice by e-mail of any new citations to an important document.

Citators play a particularly vital role in case research, where they are used to determine that a decision is still "good law." This role will be discussed more fully in Chapter 3.

§ 1–7.   Handling a Research Project

A research project usually requires you to answer a specific question by applying a general legal principle to a particular set of facts. It often involves several distinct steps: coming up to speed on the law governing a situation, searching for the specific rules that apply, making sure your information is current, and knowing when to stop researching.

a. First Steps

The first step in most research projects is to determine the legal issues in a factual situation. Before looking anywhere, step back and study the problem. What are the material facts and issues that may be important in finding the relevant law? What is the relationship between the people involved? Are they, for example, employer/employee or parties to a contract? When did the significant events occur? If possible, determine whether the jurisdictional focus is federal or state.

Your goal is to determine how the law will apply to the specific facts of your case. To do this, generally you look for cases, statutes, or other documents addressing the legal issues in your case, and involving similar or analogous facts. It's important to formulate tentative issues at the outset, but also to be prepared to revise your statement of the issues as research progresses and you learn more about the legal background.

Some preliminary research is usually needed to understand the context of a particular problem and to get some sense of the terminology and rules of an area of law. Without knowing the parameters of a particular field, you cannot understand the significance of material found and appreciate the nuances.

It is often best to begin research by going to a trustworthy secondary source, such as a legal treatise or a law review article. Primary sources such as statutes and cases can be confusing, ambiguously worded documents. Secondary materials are usually more straightforward and try to explain the law. They summarize the basic rules and the leading authorities and place them in context, allowing you to select the most promising primary sources to pursue.

When researching an issue that fits within a traditional area of legal doctrine, begin by consulting a subject treatise or hornbook in the area. A treatise explains the major issues and terminology, and provides a context in which analogous matters are raised or considered. The names of some of the most famous treatises, such as *Corbin on Contracts* or

Wright & Miller's *Federal Practice and Procedure*, are familiar to most law students, and works in other areas can be found by using a law library's online catalog, by asking a reference librarian, or by exploring the resources available through the major online services.

If no treatise is available, a legal encyclopedia such as *American Jurisprudence 2d* or *Corpus Juris Secundum* can be a useful first step. (Both of these encyclopedias are on Westlaw; Lexis has *American Jurisprudence 2d*.) Like a treatise, an encyclopedia outlines basic legal rules and has extensive references to court decisions. A treatise or encyclopedia may not address a specific situation, but it provides the general framework in which to place the facts and legal issues.

Law review articles are particularly useful starting points when researching a new or developing area of law that may not be very well covered in treatises or encyclopedias. Westlaw and Lexis have vast collections of law review articles, and Google Scholar can also be a good starting point. Sources such as legal newspapers, newsletters, and blogs are even more current than law reviews.

This early stage of the research process is also a good point at which to use free Internet sites such as search engines or Wikipedia (www.wikipedia.org). At this point you are looking for background information and not definitive answers or citable authority, so a free and readily accessible website can be a real boon. A general source such as Wikipedia, while not authoritative, can provide basic facts as well as leads to more in-depth resources.

Most researchers begin their research online, but resources such as treatises and encyclopedias may actually be easier to understand in print. Books can make it simpler to scan headings, get an overview of an area, and learn about related issues.

The most difficult part of many research projects is finding the first piece of relevant information. Once one document is found, it often leads to a number of other sources. Cases cite earlier cases as authority; a statute's notes provide useful leads to decisions, legislative history documents, and secondary sources; and treatises and law review articles cite a wide variety of sources.

b. *In-Depth Research*

Once you gain background knowledge of an area, you can use that knowledge to guide the thorough research needed to find all of the law most relevant to your specific set of facts.

Several research tools discussed in this book are designed for in-depth research. Annotated codes, for example, not only have the texts of current statutes, but also lead directly to most of the other relevant primary sources and often have references to secondary sources as well. Specialized services in areas such as securities or taxation often combine the statutory text with editorial explanatory notes.

West key numbers (on Westlaw or in digests), Lexis topics, and *ALR* annotations expand on keyword searches by grouping cases together by topic whether or not they use the same terminology. They are valuable resources for finding situations with different facts but similar legal issues.

Once you know the contours of a legal issue, you have the background necessary to talk to experts in the area. The most current information is not always available in print or online. Sometimes an e-mail or telephone call will uncover information that couldn't be found through ordinary research methods. Government agencies and professional associations are staffed with experts who can answer questions, provide invaluable references, or send hard-to-find documents. Do your homework first, and make sure that the information isn't posted on the organization's website.

In-depth research may require several approaches. At first you may seem to be facing a blank wall, or think you have found everything there is to be found. Try rephrasing the question and running searches using new terminology. Taking a break from the project for a few hours or talking to colleagues may lead you to fresh insights.

c. Having Current Information

An essential part of legal research is verifying that the information you've found is current. You must make sure that your sources are still in force and "good law." No research is complete unless you have checked the latest supplements, searched current-awareness sources for new developments, and determined the status of cases and statutes to be relied upon.

There are at least two distinct aspects to making sure that your information and knowledge are current. The first is checking the sources on which you're relying to answer a specific research question. Citators confirm the validity of precedent and lead you to more current information. They provide signals indicating that the precedential value of cases might be affected by subsequent decisions or other developments, and they alert you to recent documents that might provide clarification or new perspectives.

The second aspect of being up to date is a more general confidence and comes with expertise in a particular subject area. Monitoring new developments on a regular basis, by reading newsletters, trade magazines, and blogs, ensures that you won't be blindsided by a new case or regulation that affects your clients.

d. Completing a Project

Knowing when to stop researching can be just as difficult as knowing where to begin. In every research situation, however, there comes a time when it is necessary to synthesize the information you have found and produce the required memorandum, brief, or opinion letter.

Sometimes the limits to research are set by the nature of the project. An assignment may be limited to a specified number of hours or a certain amount of money. If so, the ability to find information quickly and accurately is essential.

If there is no preset limit to the amount of research to be done, it is up to you to determine when you are finished. You must do enough research to be confident that your work is based on information that is comprehensive and current. The surest way to achieve this confidence is to try several different approaches to the research problem. If a review of the secondary literature, a digest search, and online queries produce different conclusions, more research is needed. When these various approaches lead to the same primary sources and a single conclusion, you can be more confident that a key piece of information has not eluded you.

As we will see in the following chapters, the law has a voluminous literature and a wide range of research resources. Learning to use these resources requires patience and effort, but in time you will become aware of the different functions they serve, their strengths and weaknesses, and the ways they fit together. Experience in their use will give you the confidence that you are finding all the documents and information you need.

CHAPTER 2

BACKGROUND AND ANALYSIS

Images of some resources discussed in this chapter are at **libguides.law.virginia.edu/nutshell12/ch2**

---

§ 2–1. Introduction

Primary sources of law—such as constitutional provisions, legislative enactments, and judicial decisions—determine legal rights and govern procedures. Primary sources, however, are difficult places in which to find answers at the beginning of a research project. Secondary sources that explain and analyze governing legal doctrines make primary sources more accessible and should serve as launching pads for most research projects.

This chapter focuses on major resources that are most likely to be helpful when starting research. Encyclopedias, treatises, *Restatements*, and law review articles set forth established legal doctrine, explain its nuances, and help you understand how a problem fits into the doctrinal structure. They can introduce a new area of law or refresh your recollection of a familiar area.

The different types of secondary sources fit varying research needs. Some treatises and law review articles contain influential insights that can shape law reform or stimulate new legislation. Other sources are more practical and provide a straight-forward overview of the law without advocating changes. Some are written primarily for law students and spell out basic doctrines, while others are designed for practicing lawyers and have guidelines and forms to simplify common procedures.

Most secondary sources include references to the primary sources needed for further research. They discuss the leading cases and major statutes, and contain extensive footnotes leading directly to these and numerous other sources. These footnote references may appear to be among the more mundane aspects of a secondary source, but for the researcher they are invaluable.

Secondary legal literature is much broader than the basic resources discussed in this chapter, and additional specialized materials will be discussed in later chapters. These general works, however, can provide a solid basis for successful research of most legal issues.

§ 2–2. Overviews

There is nothing wrong with doing preliminary research in a free online resource such as Wikipedia (www.wikipedia.org), as long as you recognize that it is only a starting point. Further research in legal resources will be necessary to find the more sophisticated detail and supporting documentation required for legal analysis.

A number of printed and online reference works focus on coverage of legal issues. Some, such as *Encyclopedia of Crime and Justice* (Joshua Dressler ed., 2d ed. 2002), or *Encyclopedia of the American Constitution* (Leonard W. Levy & Kenneth L. Karst eds., 2d ed. 2000), are well-respected interdisciplinary treatments with contributions from legal scholars, historians, and political scientists. *Oxford Companion to American Law* (Kermit L. Hall ed., 2002) is a one-volume work covering a broad range of major legal concepts, institutions, cases, and historical figures, with most articles accompanied by references for further reading. *The New Oxford Companion to Law* (Peter Cane & Joanne Conaghan eds., 2008) focuses primarily on British institutions and legal history, but it also covers American topics and contains a great deal of useful information on our common law heritage.

Works such as these provide a broad perspective on legal issues and can place these issues in the context of other political or societal concerns. They generally will not answer more specific questions about particular legal situations, however, and they contain references to relatively few primary sources.

More detailed coverage is found in works designed specifically for lawyers and law students.

§ 2–3. Legal Encyclopedias

Legal encyclopedias are not simply general encyclopedias about legal topics, but works that attempt to describe systematically the entire body of legal doctrine. Instead of thousands of articles on specific factual topics, they have a few hundred articles covering broad areas such as constitutional law or criminal law.

Encyclopedias are generally not viewed as persuasive secondary authority, but rather as introductory surveys and as case-finding tools. They are relatively slow to reflect changes in the law or to cover significant trends in developing areas. Also, in most instances, legal encyclopedias tend to emphasize case law over statutes and regulations, and they rarely examine the historical or societal aspects of the rules they discuss. Unlike law review articles or scholarly treatises, they simply summarize legal doctrine without criticism or suggestions for improvement.

a. American Jurisprudence 2d *and* Corpus Juris Secundum

Two national encyclopedias attempt to provide comprehensive outlines of state and federal legal doctrine. These were once competing works but both are now published by Thomson Reuters: *American Jurisprudence 2d* (*Am. Jur. 2d*) and *Corpus Juris Secundum* (*C.J.S.*). Each of these sets contains more than 140 volumes, with articles on more than 400 broad legal topics. Some articles, such as "Cemeteries" or "Dead Bodies," are narrowly defined and span just a few dozen pages, but articles on topics as broad as "Corporations" or "Evidence" can occupy several volumes. Each article is divided into numbered sections and begins with a section-by-section outline of its contents and an explanation of its scope.

Westlaw has both encyclopedias, and *Am. Jur. 2d* is also available through Lexis. Each section is treated as a separate document, but tables of contents make it possible to see how a particular section fits in a broader context. You can begin by browsing through the table of contents, or you can search and then link from a retrieved section to the outline for its article.

Am. Jur. 2d and *C.J.S.* are quite similar, but there are differences between these two works. *C.J.S.* begins each section or subsection with a concise "black letter" statement of the general legal principle, and it generally has more footnotes than *Am. Jur. 2d*. The discussion in *Am. Jur. 2d* tends to focus a bit more on federal law, while *C.J.S.* seeks to provide an overall synthesis of state law and usually cites more state cases than *Am. Jur. 2d*. The text in both works is accompanied by copious footnotes to court decisions and occasional references to federal statutes and uniform laws. Neither work cites state statutes; even when expressly discussing state statutory provisions, the footnotes refer to cases that cite these statutes. When searching for references to cases, it's often worth checking both encyclopedias. They may cover the same issue with no overlap in the cases they cite.

Am. Jur. 2d and *C.J.S.* also contain references to other case-finding materials. Both encyclopedias provide relevant *key numbers*, classifications that can be used to find cases on Westlaw or in West digests. *Am. Jur. 2d* also includes references to *American Law Reports* (*ALR*) annotations, which describe and analyze cases on specific topics. Digests and *ALR* will be discussed in Chapter 3 with other case-finding tools.

The basic means of access to the print encyclopedias are the multivolume indexes published annually for each set. Most legal encyclopedia articles are very lengthy and cover broad areas of legal doctrine, so a pinpoint reference from the index usually saves considerable time. The indexes are very detailed, and finding the right section may require patience and flexibility. You may need to rethink your terms or follow cross-references.

Westlaw has searchable access to the indexes for both encyclopedias, and also allows you to restrict a keyword search to terms in section headings through an Advanced Search. It uses the field *PR* or *Preliminary* for words in the titles of articles and subdivisions, and the field *TI* or *Title* for words in individual section headings. On Lexis, you can use the Advanced Search screen's *Title* segment to limit a search to section headings. Limiting a search to headings is often a productive way to zero in on the most relevant material.

You can also find relevant *Am. Jur. 2d* and *C.J.S.* sections through Westlaw Citing References, as both encyclopedias are listed as citing secondary sources for any case or federal statute they mention. Shepard's on Lexis covers other secondary sources, but not these national encyclopedias.

b. Jurisdictional Encyclopedias

Most of the larger states have multivolume encyclopedias specifically focusing on the law of those jurisdictions. These state encyclopedias often do a better job of tying together statutory and case law than the national encyclopedias. While not generally viewed as authoritative, they can provide both a good general overview of state law and footnotes leading to many primary sources.

Each of these works is a comprehensive summary of its state's legal doctrine, organized like *Am. Jur. 2d* or *C.J.S.* into several hundred alphabetically arranged articles and regularly updated by annual supplements and revised volumes. Depending on its publisher, each state encyclopedia is available through either Westlaw or Lexis as well as in print.

Many states have other reference works that summarize and explain their law, although not necessarily made up of alphabetically arranged articles like the national encyclopedias. Sets such as *Kentucky Jurisprudence* and *Massachusetts Practice*, for example, contain separate volumes for doctrinal areas such as criminal procedure, domestic relations, and evidence. They may not cover all legal topics comprehensively, but they do address most major areas. The state research guides listed in Appendix A on pages 291–302 can help you identify available resources.

Thomson Reuters also publishes, in print and on Westlaw, an encyclopedia focusing specifically on federal law, *Federal Procedure, Lawyers' Edition*. It emphasizes procedural issues in civil, criminal and administrative proceedings, but many of its chapters also discuss matters of substantive federal law. Because it deals exclusively with federal law rather than attempting to generalize about fifty state jurisdictions, it is often more precise and useful than *Am. Jur. 2d* or *C.J.S.* and includes helpful pointers for federal practice.

§ 2–4. Texts and Treatises

For centuries, legal treatises have played a vital role in legal research. They analyze the changing common law and also influence its development. By synthesizing decisions and statutes, treatises help to impose order on the chaos of individual precedents. Although they have no binding authority, some are written by scholars of outstanding reputation and are frequently cited by the courts.

Types of Law Books. While there is no clear demarcation between different types of texts, they can be grouped into several general categories:

• Scholarly treatises (e.g., *Moore's Federal Practice*, *Wigmore on Evidence*) have exhaustive coverage of specific subjects. A treatise is similar to an encyclopedia in that it methodically outlines the basic aspects of legal doctrine, but its focus on a specific subject means that a treatise usually has greater depth and insight. Many of the original multivolume treatises were written by leading scholars (such as James William Moore or John H. Wigmore), but a number of titles are now produced by editorial staffs at publishing companies. The traditional treatise is a multivolume work covering a broad area of legal doctrine such as contracts or trusts. Modern treatises tend to focus on increasingly narrow areas of law, and many are just one or two volumes. Treatises are the texts most likely to be available through one of the major online services. Some are still available only in print, but others, such as *Bloomberg Law: Bankruptcy Treatise*, are online only.

• Hornbooks and law school texts are written primarily for a student audience but can be of value to anyone seeking an overview of a doctrinal area. These are distinct from *casebooks*, designed as teaching tools, which reprint cases for discussion and tend to have a less straightforward summary of legal doctrine. There is no clear line distinguishing hornbooks from treatises. Some hornbooks, such as *McCormick on Evidence* or *Wright on Federal Courts*, are highly respected and are frequently cited as authority in court decisions and law review articles. Other works, such as West Academic's Nutshell Series, are meant primarily as law school study guides and are rarely cited by judges or scholars. Works designed for law students are unlikely to be available online through the major services, but some schools have online subscriptions to West Academic Study Aids.

• Practitioners' handbooks and manuals, many published by organizations such as the Practising Law Institute (PLI) and state bar associations, are less useful for students but can be invaluable to practicing lawyers. They often include chapters on specific issues by leading practitioners in an area, and frequently have features such as checklists and sample forms designed to simplify routine aspects of law practice. Works focusing on the law of a specific state may help you quickly determine the rules in force and lead you to relevant primary sources. Many of these works are available online as well as in print.

• Scholarly monographs on relatively narrow topics, such as Risa Goluboff's *Vagrant Nation: Police Power, Constitutional Change and the Making of the 1960s*, can help you understand the history or policy background of a particular area. Because they are generally not exhaustive in their coverage of doctrinal issues and are rarely updated on a regular basis, such works are usually not the best sources for current research leads. Many are published as e-books, but they are unlikely to be available online through services such as Westlaw or Lexis.

• Self-help publications, such as those published by Nolo Press (e.g., *How to Get a*

Green Card or *Patent It Yourself*), can be good starting points and often have clear introductions to areas of law. They may oversimplify complex issues, however, and they tend to include fewer leads to primary sources than works written for law students or lawyers. Very few self-help works are included in the major online services, but e-books are usually available through the publishers' websites.

For any of these publications to be reliable for coverage of current legal issues, it must be regularly updated to reflect changes in the law promptly and accurately. When using a text in any format, you should be aware of how current it is and look for more recent authority as necessary. In print, check the date of the most recent edition or supplement; online, look for an information icon or "Currency" link. An outdated text may be of historical or intellectual interest, but it is not reliable as a statement of today's law.

Finding Texts and Treatises. There are several ways to identify relevant and useful texts, including directories in the online services, your local law library's catalog, and guides and bibliographies. Major texts and treatises are most commonly accessed online, but you shouldn't limit yourself to materials available from the major services.

Hundreds of treatises and other texts are available from Westlaw, Lexis, and Bloomberg Law. These sources are included in global search results, but you should also browse to learn what resources are available. A bit of exploring and familiarity with resources can pay dividends when you know where to turn in future research projects. This is particularly true with treatises; unlike materials such as case law, no service has comprehensive coverage. Each has works published by specific companies and not others, and there is very little overlap in coverage.

Westlaw's broad treatise collections include major works such as Rotunda & Nowak's *Treatise on Constitutional Law* and Wright & Miller's *Federal Practice and Procedure*. Clicking on Secondary Sources and then Texts & Treatises allows you to scan the list of titles in a topical area. You can search all the texts in an area or choose a particular title to search or browse.

Lexis has hundreds of Matthew Bender texts and treatises, including *Chisum on Patents*, *Collier on Bankruptcy*, and *Immigration Law and Procedure*, as well as selected works from other publishers. To learn what's available, you can browse sources by practice area, and narrow the result to secondary materials and then treatises. The resulting list includes options to search or browse tables of contents.

Bloomberg Law has numerous practitioners' manuals, including many published by the American Bar Association and the Practising Law Institute. Of particular value are major Bloomberg BNA publications such as *Employment Discrimination Law* and *Supreme Court Practice*, as well as the online-only *Bloomberg Law: Bankruptcy Treatise* noted earlier. The main screen includes a Books & Treatises link, which leads to listings by publisher. Treatises can be found by subject in ten major subject areas by using one of the Practice Centers links.

Once you have found a relevant treatise section using a search, unless you are very familiar with the subject area or looking only for very specific information you should usually browse through the table of contents to explore related material. If you read only the individual retrieved sections, you'll learn little about the contours in that area of law.

It can be difficult when browsing titles in an online service to distinguish between a major comprehensive work and a slim volume, so when working in an unfamiliar area it is often helpful to evaluate texts in print. A law library's online catalog is a basic starting place for finding print texts and treatises. A title keyword search can be used initially to find a few relevant works, but you will want to go beyond keywords and use the subject headings for more comprehensive research. Standardized subject headings mean that works on similar topics are grouped together no matter what words are used in their titles. A hyperlink from one work's subject heading can quickly retrieve a list of other items in the catalog with the same heading.

Most online catalogs have an "advanced search" or "expanded search" screen that allows you to search for a combination of terms in specific fields. You can use this to find a particular work by a prolific author, for example, or to limit a search to a specific date range. Other catalogs let you filter results by date or library collection once a search is completed. These options can be particularly useful if a general keyword search turns up an unmanageably large number of publications.

Treatises are often cited in cases and law review articles, and following leads provided by these sources is usually a reliable way to find works that are considered well-reasoned and reputable. You can find highly esteemed treatises by searching in case or journal databases (e.g., "leading w/2 treatise w/5 contracts") or simply noting the treatises that are cited repeatedly by judges or law professors. Recommendations from professors or senior attorneys may also help you identify the most reliable and influential sources.

The most comprehensive subject guide to current treatises is found in Kendall Svengalis's annual *Legal Information Buyer's Guide and Reference Manual*. A 400-page chapter on treatises has annotated listings in about sixty subject areas, with useful information about the scope and expense of the works listed. A shorter list of major treatises and hornbooks is included in this volume, as Appendix B on pages 303–321.

Treatises and practice materials focusing on the law of particular jurisdictions are usually listed or described in state legal research guides (listed in Appendix A at pages 291–302), and *State Practice Materials: Annotated Bibliographies* (Frank G. Houdek ed., 2002–date; available on HeinOnline) covers treatises by subject for about forty states.

Evaluating Texts. Part of the process of using a text for the first time is deciding whether it is a resource you will want to return to for further research. Even without expertise in a subject area, you can ask several questions when encountering a new work:

— What is its purpose and intended audience? Is it written for experienced specialists or a more general readership?

— How is it organized, and what is its scope? Does it cover too broad an area for your purposes, or does it focus on issues that don't concern you?

— What is the reputation of the author? Has she written other texts or articles in this area?

— How useful are features such as the work's index, tables and footnotes? Do they lead effectively to relevant passages in the work and to other resources?

— Is the work supplemented or updated in an adequate and timely manner?

Ultimately the deciding factor in determining whether you will turn to a text a second time is whether it helped answer your question. Did it clarify matters and provide fruitful research leads? A reliable treatise allows you to explore an unfamiliar area with the help of an experienced and insightful guide. As your familiarity in a particular area of law grows, you will develop a sense of which sources are best for background information, for working through a complicated legal issue, or for references to further research sources.

§ 2–5.   *Restatements of the Law*

Some of the most important commentaries on American law are the series called *Restatements of the Law*, published by the American Law Institute (ALI). The *Restatements* attempt to organize and articulate the rules in selected subject fields. They are drafted by respected scholars and jurists, and are perhaps more persuasive to courts than any other secondary material. Courts and legislatures sometimes explicitly adopt *Restatement* provisions as correct statements of the law.

The *Restatements* have excellent summaries of basic doctrines, useful both for students learning an area of law and for lawyers seeking to apply the law to novel issues arising in practice. A *Restatement* is divided into sections, each of which contains a concise "black letter" statement of law, followed by explanatory comments and illustrations of particular examples and variations on the general proposition. Reporter's Notes provide background information on the section's development, and appendices contain annotations of court decisions that have applied or interpreted each section.

Each *Restatement* covers a distinct area of law. Topics covered to date include agency, conflict of laws, contracts, employment law, foreign relations law, judgments, the law governing lawyers, property, restitution and unjust enrichment, suretyship and guaranty, torts, trusts, and unfair competition. The *Restatements* have been published in three series since 1932, and some of these topics have been considered and restated more than once as the law develops and changes.

The ALI has also published a series of *Principles*, which are less firmly based on existing case law than *Restatements* and are more explicitly recommendations for change, about aggregate litigation, corporate governance, family law, intellectual property, and software contracts. Other *Restatement* and *Principles* projects are in various stages of development.

The process of drafting a *Restatement* or *Principles* is a long one, usually involving the publication of several preliminary and tentative drafts. Changes in the process can show the development of consensus, or differences of opinion, about a legal doctrine.

The *Restatements* and *Principles*, including some drafts, are available on both Westlaw and Lexis. HeinOnline has an American Law Institute collection with PDF versions of the *Restatements* and *Principles*, including drafts, as well as other ALI materials such as annual reports and proceedings. The American Law Institute website (www.ali.org) has information on publications and pending projects.

§ 2–6. Law Reviews

The academic legal journals known as law reviews are the major forum through which legal academics debate and develop legal theories. Most law review articles have two features that make them invaluable in research. They generally begin with an introductory overview of the area of law that summarizes the relevant doctrine and literature, and they are usually replete with footnotes citing to primary sources and to other secondary sources.

Unlike journals in most scholarly disciplines, law reviews are edited by students rather than established scholars and serve as educational tools for their editors as well as a forum for discussion of legal developments and theories. A law review issue usually follows a fairly standard format, containing lengthy *articles* and shorter *essays* by professors and lawyers followed by *comments* or *notes* by students. The articles and essays are more influential, but the student contributions can also be valuable in research if they summarize the law well and have footnotes with useful leads to other sources.

Law review articles differ from more general works such as legal encyclopedias and treatises in several ways. Articles are often written on recent cases and statutes, so they are among the best resources for researching newly developing areas of law. They often advocate changes in the legal system and generally have a less neutral perspective than other sources. Unlike secondary sources such as encyclopedias and treatises, law review articles are not updated after they are published.

Practically every law school approved by the American Bar Association has a general law review that publishes articles on a wide range of topics. Most schools also have additional journals on specialized subjects, with some publishing a dozen or more titles. Most subject-specific journals are student-edited, but a few, such as *Florida Tax Review* and *Supreme*

Court Review, are edited by law school faculty. The term "law review" generally encompasses all of these academic legal journals.

Most national and state bar associations publish monthly or quarterly magazines with shorter articles and more emphasis on graphics and readability. Even a glossy magazine, however, may contain valuable articles on topics of current interest in its jurisdiction. Because they are written for lawyers, even short articles generally have footnotes with references to cases, code provisions, and other sources.

a. Westlaw and Lexis

Numerous online services provide access to primary sources such as cases and statutes, but only a few offer comprehensive coverage of law review articles. Westlaw and Lexis both have the full text of more than eight hundred law reviews and journals, with coverage for some reviews extending from the early 1980s or earlier and many more beginning in the 1990s.

A full-text search can be used to pinpoint discussion or footnotes using any specific combination of words, including phrases, case names, or titles of other articles or books. Even if no article directly on point is found, articles on related topics may include references to more relevant sources, including treatises or journal volumes that are not themselves online.

Because the services contain thousands of lengthy articles, an advanced search limited to the Title field may lead to a smaller but more relevant group of documents. You can also focus retrieval by using proximity connectors and the Term Frequency feature, and you can use Westlaw's Author field to find articles by particular scholars.

When search results are listed by relevance rather than by date, be careful not to rely on outdated articles or miss important recent contributions. One way to make sure that your research is current once you find a relevant article is to click on its Citing References tab in Westlaw or its Shepardize link in Lexis. Even if the first article you find is several years old, these tools give you an easy way to find more recent articles that may be relevant to your research.

b. *HeinOnline*

Westlaw and Lexis have the full text of articles, but they cannot display images and other graphic material. To see the text of footnotes requires hovering over or clicking on the note number, which can be a time-consuming process when looking for research leads. (Bloomberg Law features page images for some, but not all, journals.) HeinOnline, on the other hand, has digitized images from the printed journal issues, including graphics in the original and footnotes at the bottom of each page for convenient access.

HeinOnline covers more than two thousand journals, and its retrospective coverage extends back to the very first volumes of most journals in its database. The *University of Pennsylvania Law Review*, for example, is included back to 1852, when it began publication as the *American Law Register*. This full-text access to older law reviews makes HeinOnline particularly valuable in legal history research, but for most titles it includes the most recently published issues as well.

HeinOnline offers full-text searching of its journals, with an Advanced Search screen providing options to search for words or phrases in Author, Title, or Text fields and to limit a search to specific subjects, journals, or dates. A Citation Navigator allows you to retrieve articles by citation. Westlaw and Lexis generally have more powerful search options to find recent law review articles, and HeinOnline is most effective for historical research or document retrieval.

c. Periodical Indexes

Full-text searching can sometimes have drawbacks. Even with relevance ranking, keyword searches can retrieve extraneous articles that use the search terms but do not focus on a particular subject. Limiting a search to title keywords can help, but not all articles have very descriptive or informative titles. Periodical indexes that narrow retrieval to articles more specifically on point remain useful resources, especially when links lead directly from index entries to the full text of articles.

Two general indexes to English-language legal periodical literature are available, both in print and online. *Index to Legal Periodicals and Books* (*ILP*) is available from EBSCOhost (www.ebscohost.com), and to some subscribers through other online services. LegalTrac is part of the Gale Group's InfoTrac service (find.galegroup.com). It is called Legal Resource Index (LRI) on Westlaw and Lexis, and its print version is *Current Law Index*. Each of these indexes covers more than a thousand law reviews and periodicals, with coverage back to the early 1980s, and both include the full text of many of the articles indexed. EBSCOhost also has an Index to Legal Periodicals Retrospective database, cumulating entries from older index volumes from 1908 to 1981.

Both LegalTrac and *ILP* offer several search approaches as well as subject indexing, making it easy to find relevant articles. LegalTrac uses detailed Library of Congress subjects with subheadings and cross-references, while *ILP* generally has fewer, broader subjects. Each approach has advantages; sometimes your research may have a very specific focus, while at other times a broader survey is needed. Once you find one relevant article, clicking on its subject headings links you to other articles on related topics.

Even for the articles not available from *ILP* or LegalTrac in full text, many libraries offer "link resolvers" that lead directly from an index entry to the full text in HeinOnline or other resources. This method combines the best of both research worlds: expert indexing to ensure that relevant articles aren't missed, and immediate online access to the text.

d. Other Resources

Westlaw, Lexis, and HeinOnline are the most thorough collections of law review articles, but they are not the only available resources. Bloomberg Law has a limited collection of law reviews, in some instances with only very recent coverage. For some law reviews, however, it offers PDF images of the original printed version.

Google Scholar (scholar.google.com) can be a free and convenient place to begin research. It provides full-text access to thousands of law review articles. Access to the full text of some articles is free, but for others it depends on whether your institution subscribes to resources such as HeinOnline or JSTOR. Google Scholar listings also offer ways to expand research with links to more recent works citing the listed article ("Cited by") and articles with similar terms ("Related Articles").

A growing number of law reviews now provide free access to recent articles on their websites, although some still feature only tables of contents or abstracts and many are not fully up to date. Several law reviews also feature shorter pieces available only electronically, in online supplements with titles like *In Brief* or *Sidebar*. In addition, many recent articles and working papers are available through scholarship repositories such as Berkeley Electronic Press (www.bepress.com) and Social Science Research Network (SSRN) (www.ssrn.com).

References to law review articles are often found in the process of researching primary sources such as case law or statutes. The citing references for cases and statutes include law review articles, and annotated statutory codes often contain lists of relevant articles. These approaches will be discussed in the following chapters, with other aspects of case and statutory research.

Law reviews and journals are not the only types of legal periodicals. More specialized and practice-oriented sources such as legal newspapers and newsletters, as well as resources for historical research and current scholarship, are considered in Chapter 8.

CHAPTER 3

CASE LAW

***Images of some resources discussed in this chapter
are at* libguides.law.virginia.edu/nutshell12/ch3**

---

§ 3–1.   Introduction

Reports of judicial decisions are among the most important sources of legal authority in the common law system. Over the course of time, judges shape legal doctrines to address the complex issues of our changing society. Legislative enactments cover an ever broader range of issues, but even a statute that appears straightforward must be read in light of the court decisions that construe and apply its provisions.

Court Systems. To use cases effectively, it is necessary to understand the hierarchical structure of the American judicial system. The precedential value of a decision is determined in large part by a court's place in this hierarchy. Decisions from a higher court in a jurisdiction are *binding* or *mandatory authority*, and must be followed by a lower court in the same jurisdiction. Decisions from courts in other jurisdictions are not binding, but a court in another state may have considered a situation similar to that in issue and may provide *persuasive authority*.

Litigation usually begins in a *trial court*, the lowest level of the hierarchy. In the trial court, *issues of fact* (e.g., whether a "Beware of Dog" sign was posted) are decided by the fact finder, either the judge or a jury. These factual findings are binding on the parties and cannot be appealed. *Issues of law* (e.g., whether such a sign limits a dog owner's liability for injuries) are decided by the judge, and a party who disagrees with these rulings can appeal them to a higher court.

Appeals from trial court decisions are generally taken to an *intermediate appellate court* (the U.S. Courts of Appeals and similar state tribunals). An appellate court usually consists of a panel of three or more judges, who confer and vote on the issues after considering written briefs and oral argument. One of the judges writes a *majority opinion* summarizing the question and stating the court's holding. In some cases the court issues a *per curiam* opinion that is not attributed to any individual judge. A judge who agrees with the holding of a case but not for the reasons expressed by the majority may write a separate *concurring opinion* outlining her views. A judge who disagrees with the holding may write a *dissenting opinion*. Only a majority or per curiam opinion is binding authority.

The *court of last resort* in each jurisdiction (called the Supreme Court in the federal system and in most states) usually reviews cases from the intermediate appellate courts, but may take appeals directly from trial courts. Unlike other appellate courts, most courts of last resort have discretion in deciding which cases they will hear. Their role in the judicial system is not to resolve every individual dispute, but rather to establish rules, review legislative and administrative acts, and resolve differences among intermediate appellate courts. A court of last resort's decisions on issues of law are binding on all courts within its jurisdiction.

Daniel John Meador & Gregory Mitchell, *American Courts* (3d ed. 2009) is one of the more concise introductory works on the role of judges in deciding cases and creating legal doctrine. Longer treatments useful for background reading and references to other sources include Lawrence Baum, *American Courts: Process and Policy* (7th ed. 2013) and Robert A. Carp et al., *Judicial Process in America* (9th ed. 2014).

Publication of Cases. Case law generally consists of the decisions of courts of last resort and intermediate appellate courts on issues of law. Trial court decisions on issues of fact have no precedential effect and usually do not even result in written judicial opinions. A jury verdict at the end of a trial, for example, produces no published decision unless the judge rules on a motion challenging the verdict on legal grounds. Some trial court decisions on issues of law are published, but they have less precedential value than appellate court decisions. Selected intermediate appellate court decisions and nearly all decisions from courts of last resort are published both in print and online.

A bit of history may help in understanding the publication of cases. Early American judges and lawyers relied on English precedents, since the first published volume of American decisions, *Kirby's Reports* in Connecticut, did not appear until 1789. Reports from other states and from the new federal courts soon followed. Many of these early reports were cited by the names of their editors and are known as *nominative reports*.

Official series of court reports began in several states in the early 1800s. As the country grew in the 19th century, the number of reported decisions increased dramatically. In 1879, John B. West launched the *North Western Reporter*, publishing new decisions of five Midwestern states much more quickly than the official reports. By 1887, West published cases from every state and the federal system, in what became known as the National Reporter System. These reporters, now published by Thomson Reuters, are the most widely accepted source for citations to court opinions.

New decisions are available online much sooner than they are published in print, from both commercial services and court websites. Most researchers find and read cases online instead of in printed reports, but cases are still identified by citations to the published volumes. Generally, only cases unavailable in print are cited to online sources.

The first appearance of a new decision is the official *slip opinion*, an individually paginated copy of a single decision that is usually available free from the court website. Slip opinions, however, have two major drawbacks. First, they rarely have editorial enhancements summarizing the court's decision and facilitating research. Second, they must be cited by docket number and date rather than to a permanent published source. Some jurisdictions have sought to ameliorate this second problem by assigning *public domain citations* to their recent cases. Opinions are numbered as they are issued, and in some states each paragraph is numbered so that a particular point in an opinion can be identified, as in the Supreme Court of Montana case of *State v. Olson*, 2014 MT 8, ¶ 31.

Later versions of decisions provide the editorial summaries and page citations that slip opinions lack. In print, cases usually appear first in pamphlets known as *advance sheets*, containing a number of decisions paginated in a continuous sequence, and then in bound volumes consolidating the contents of several advance sheets. Volumes are numbered consecutively, often in more than one successive series. If a reporter is in a second, third, or fourth series, that must be indicated in its citation in order to distinguish it from the same volume number in another series.

Most court reports include editorial features that make it easier to find and understand the decisions. In West's National Reporter System series, each case is prefaced with a brief summary of its holding, called a *synopsis*, and with numbered editorial abstracts, or *headnotes*, of the specific legal issues.

It is important to remember that the synopsis and headnotes are not prepared by the court and should not be cited or relied upon as authoritative. They also may cover topics discussed in dictum, sometimes even in footnotes, rather than the case's holding. You need to read the opinion to determine the court's holding, and to cite the text in the opinion rather than a synopsis or headnote.

Case Research. For the doctrine of precedent to operate effectively, lawyers must be able to find cases that control or influence a court's decision-making. You are looking for decisions from courts that have binding or persuasive precedent in your jurisdiction, on topics related to the issues in your case. You are searching for cases addressing factual or legal issues similar to yours, in order to determine how their holdings apply to the specific facts of your case. You then need to determine that these cases have not been reversed, overruled, or otherwise discredited.

When researching case law, many law students tend to rely almost exclusively on online keyword searches. These searches are valuable, but they are most effective as part of a research strategy that integrates other tools and approaches. Other resources we will discuss in this chapter, such as West key numbers and *ALR* annotations, are the works of experienced editors who have analyzed cases and classified them according to the legal principles they address. These resources may at first seem more confusing than helpful, but skill in their use can yield important results, insights, and analogies that you might never find using only keyword searches. Using several different approaches will ensure that you're not missing anything and give you confidence in your results.

This chapter discusses several major tools to help you find cases and affirm their validity, but it is not exhaustive. Much of legal research revolves around finding cases, and several resources discussed in other chapters—such as treatises, law reviews, and annotated codes—are also valuable in case research.

§ 3–2. Federal Court Cases

Cases are available from a variety of printed and online sources. Even if you do most of your research online, knowing about the major series of reports in which court decisions are published can help you understand citations, assess the precedential value of decisions, and locate the specific source that *The Bluebook* or the *ALWD Guide* requires you to cite.

a. *Supreme Court of the United States*

The Supreme Court of the United States stands at the head of the judicial branch of government, and provides the definitive interpretation of the U.S. Constitution and federal statutes. Its decisions are read not only by lawyers, but also by political scientists, historians, and citizens interested in the development of social and legal policy.

The Supreme Court is the court of last resort in the federal court system. It also has the final word on federal issues raised in state courts, and it hears cases arising between states. The Court exercises tight control over its docket and has wide discretion to decline review, or to *deny a writ of certiorari* as it is called in almost all cases. The Supreme Court usually accepts for consideration only those cases that raise significant policy issues. In recent years it has issued opinions in fewer than eighty cases during its annual term, which begins on the first Monday of October and usually ends in late June.

Numerous reference works explain the history and role of the Supreme Court in the American political and legal system. Three works with comprehensive coverage of the Court's major cases, doctrinal areas, and justices are *Encyclopedia of the American Constitution* (Leonard W. Levy et al. eds., 2d ed. 2000), *Encyclopedia of the Supreme Court of the United States* (David S. Tanenhaus ed., 2008), and *Oxford Companion to the Supreme Court of the United States* (Kermit L. Hall ed., 2d ed. 2005). David G. Savage, *Guide to the U.S. Supreme Court* (5th ed. 2010) is arranged thematically rather than alphabetically, but it too explains major doctrines and discusses the history, politics, and procedures of the Court.

A wide range of statistical and historical information is available in *The Supreme Court Compendium: Data, Decisions, and Developments*

(Lee Epstein et al. eds., 5th ed. 2012). The major practical guide for lawyers bringing a case before the Court is Stephen M. Shapiro et al., *Supreme Court Practice* (10th ed. 2013), available on Bloomberg Law.

The Court's website (www.supremecourt.gov) includes a variety of information in its "About the Supreme Court" section, and numerous other websites provide background information on the Court. SCOTUSblog (www.scotusblog.com) is the leading website for the most current information on new decisions and developments in pending cases.

The Supreme Court's opinions are published in three permanent bound reporters and in a weekly newsletter. They can be found through several commercial services and free Internet sites, including the Court's own website.

U.S. Reports. The *United States Reports* (cited as U.S.) is the official edition of Supreme Court decisions. Cases appear first in slip opinion form the day they are announced, then in official advance sheets (called the "preliminary print"), and finally in the bound *U.S. Reports* volume. The Court's reporter of decisions prefaces the text of each decision with a *syllabus* summarizing the case and the Court's holding. The government publishes several volumes of *U.S. Reports* every year, but more than three years pass before a decision appears in the preliminary print and is assigned the *U.S. Reports* citation by which it is identified.

Because the published *U.S. Reports* is the official text, it can be important to have access to the cases exactly as printed. Several sites provide online access to cases in PDFs replicating the printed version. The Supreme Court website (www.supremecourt.gov) has new slip opinions as soon as they are announced and older slip opinions from several terms, although these lack the pagination necessary for citing purposes. Under the heading "Opinions—Bound Volumes," the site also has PDF files containing the final versions of *U.S. Reports* beginning with volume 502 (October Term 1991).

Cornell Law School's Legal Information Institute (LII) (www.law.cornell.edu/supct/) is another free source for PDF images of current and recent slip opinions. LII offers an e-mail notification service that delivers the syllabi of new opinions with links to the full text. HeinOnline has full coverage, with searchable PDFs of the *U.S. Reports* all the way from volume one to the most recent slip opinions.

***Supreme Court Reporter* and *Lawyers' Edition*.** Supreme Court opinions are also printed in two commercially published series, West's *Supreme Court Reporter* (cited as S. Ct.) and LexisNexis's *United States Supreme Court Reports, Lawyers' Edition* (known simply as *Lawyers' Edition*, and cited as L. Ed.). These reporters contain editorial summaries and headnotes not available in the official *U.S. Reports*, and they are the versions found in Westlaw and Lexis respectively.

The Bluebook and the *ALWD Guide* specify that a recent opinion that does not yet have a *U.S.* citation should be cited to the *Supreme Court Reporter* or *Lawyers' Edition*. Both of these sources publish decisions in paperback advance sheets within a few weeks of decision, and the page numbers are available online. The permanent bound volumes are not published until the cases appear in the *U.S. Reports* volumes, so that the commercial editions can include *star paging* references showing the page breaks in the official source.

The *Supreme Court Reporter* began in 1882, with cases from volume 106 of the *U.S. Reports*, although Westlaw includes all older Supreme Court cases as well. *Lawyers' Edition* contains all Supreme Court decisions since the Court's inception in 1790. The early *Lawyers' Edition* cases (in print or on Lexis) are particularly valuable, because the editors worked from the original manuscripts rather than the sometimes erroneous versions in the *U.S. Reports*. For some cases they include information, such as the exact date of decision, not found in the official reports.

Other Sources. While *Supreme Court Reporter* and *Lawyers' Edition* are published much sooner than the official *U.S. Reports*, there is still a lag of several weeks while editors prepare synopses and headnotes. Another publication provides access to Supreme Court cases much sooner in a newsletter format, reproducing the official slip opinions the week they are announced. This service, *The United States Law Week* (cited as U.S.L.W.), published by Bloomberg BNA, is the preferred *Bluebook* and *ALWD* citation for very recent Supreme Court decisions. *U.S. Law Week* also provides information about the Supreme Court's docket, arguments, and other developments.

Most commercial online services have complete historical coverage of Supreme Court decisions since 1790, as well as new decisions available within minutes of their release. Several free sites also provide access to the entire retrospective collection, including Google Scholar (scholar.google.com), Justia (supreme.justia.com), and Public Library of Law (www.plol.org). These sites offer a variety of search approaches and features.

b. *Lower Federal Courts*

The federal court system has grown dramatically from the thirteen District Courts and three Circuit Courts created by the Judiciary Act of 1789. The intermediate appellate courts in the federal system, the United States Courts of Appeals, are divided into thirteen circuits, consisting of the First through Eleventh Circuits (each covering several states), the District of Columbia Circuit, and the Federal Circuit. The general trial courts, the United States District Courts, are divided into ninety-four districts, with one or more in each state. There are also several specialized trial courts, such as the Bankruptcy Courts, the Court of Federal Claims, and the Court of International Trade. The U.S. Courts website has a map showing the boundaries of the circuits and districts (www.uscourts.gov/file/document/us-federal -courts-circuit-map).

The most comprehensive sources for federal court opinions are Westlaw, Lexis, and Bloomberg Law, which have complete coverage back to the beginning of the court system in 1789. *The Bluebook* and *ALWD Guide*, however, require that cases be cited to printed reporters if available there.

There is no counterpart to the *U.S. Reports* for the decisions of the U.S. Courts of Appeals and District Courts. The only officially published sources are the individual slip decisions the courts issue and post on their websites. The most thorough printed sources for lower federal court decisions are West reporters published by Thomson Reuters. In 1880, West's *Federal Reporter* began covering decisions of both circuit and district courts. More than 2,000 volumes later it is now in its third series (cited as F.3d). In 1932, with the increasing volume of litigation in the federal courts, West began another series called *Federal Supplement* (F. Supp.) for selected U.S. District Court decisions, which is now also in its third series (F. Supp. 3d). Like the *Supreme Court Reporter*, both of these reporters contain editorial synopses and headnotes with key numbers, which are invaluable tools in case research.

All three services include star paging references indicating the exact placement of specific language in a court opinion. Westlaw also has PDF images of cases, from the beginnings of both series through the most recent bound volumes.

Because these reporters cover so many different courts (unlike the *U.S. Reports*), citations to the *Federal Reporter* or *Federal Supplement* must identify the specific circuit or district in parentheses. Knowing the jurisdiction is vital in evaluating the scope and precedential value of a decision, but beginning researchers sometimes forget to include this information.

Even though the *Federal Reporter* and *Federal Supplement* publish thousands of new decisions each year, only some of the many cases the lower federal courts consider are represented in these reporter series. In an attempt to limit the proliferation of reported cases, each circuit has local court rules establishing criteria to determine whether decisions are published (e.g., establishing a new rule of law, resolving a conflict in the law, or involving issues of continuing public interest). Fewer than thirteen percent of Court of Appeals cases result in published opinions. Under the Federal Rules of Appellate Procedure, "unpublished" or "non-precedential" decisions issued after January 1, 2007, can be cited as persuasive authority, but the handling of earlier decisions varies from circuit to circuit. Some courts prohibit citation of these decisions; some allow citation, but with restrictions; and some simply limit their precedential value.

Some "unpublished" decisions are available in printed sources. West's *Federal Appendix* is a series limited to Court of Appeals decisions "not selected for publication in the *Federal Reporter*." Many more unreported decisions can be found online, but for some unreported decisions, particularly in older cases, it may be necessary to contact the clerk of the court.

Before the inception of the *Federal Reporter* in 1880, federal court decisions were issued in more than a hundred different series of nominative reports. West gathered these cases in the 1890s into a thirty-volume series called *Federal Cases*. This set incorporates over 20,000 early decisions, arranged alphabetically by case name.

Another West series, *Federal Rules Decisions* (F.R.D.), began publication in 1940 and contains U.S. District Court decisions dealing with procedural issues under the Federal Rules of Civil Procedure and the Federal Rules of Criminal Procedure. *Federal Rules Decisions* also includes judicial conference proceedings and occasional speeches or articles dealing with procedural law in the federal courts.

West also issues a number of other reporters in specialized subject fields of federal law. These include: *Military Justice Reporter* (1978–date), containing decisions of the U.S. Court of Appeals for the Armed Forces (formerly the U.S. Court of Military Appeals), as well as selected decisions of the Court of Criminal Appeals for each military branch; *Bankruptcy Reporter* (1980–date), containing Bankruptcy Court decisions and bankruptcy decisions from the U.S. District Courts; *Federal Claims Reporter* (1982–date), containing U.S. Court of Federal Claims decisions; and *Veterans Appeals Reporter* (1991–date), containing U.S. Court of Veterans Appeals decisions. West's National Reporter System does not include decisions from the U.S. Tax Court, which are published by the government in *Reports of the United States Tax Court* (1942–date) and by the major commercial tax publishers.

Federal court decisions are also printed in a variety of other sources, including commercial topical reporters designed for practitioners in specialized subject areas. Some cases appearing in these sources are not published in the *Federal Reporter* or *Federal Supplement*. Reporters in specialized areas include *American Maritime Cases* (1923–date), *Environment Reporter Cases* (1970–date), *Fair Employment Practice Cases* (1969–date), and *U.S. Patents Quarterly* (1929–date). A table in *The Bluebook* lists these and numerous other services and topical reporters.

In addition to full-text coverage of all federal court cases that appear in print in these various reporters, the online services have new decisions well before they are published and many decisions that never appear in the reporters and are otherwise available only as slip opinions. As a result, many recent cases are cited by docket number and online source rather than to a printed reporter. *United States v. Cohen*, No. WDQ–14–0130, 2015 WL 2261661 (D. Md. May 7, 2015), is an example of a case available on Westlaw but not in print. The same case is also available on Lexis at 2015 U.S. Dist. LEXIS 60840, and on Bloomberg Law at 2015 BL 135325.

Online sources other than Westlaw, Lexis, or Bloomberg Law also have broad, although not comprehensive, coverage of federal court decisions. Subscription services such as Casemaker and Fastcase have more than sixty years of Court of Appeals and District Court decisions. Free sources include Google Scholar (scholar.google.com) and Justia (www.justia.com), with Court of Appeals and District Court decisions since 1924, and Public Library of Law, with appellate cases since 1950. This coverage may not be as useful for exhaustive historical research, but it is sufficient for almost any modern legal inquiry. The U.S. Government Publishing Office (www.gpo.gov/fdsys/) has a United States Courts Opinions collection, with recent opinions from the Courts of Appeals, District Courts, and Bankruptcy Courts, and selected coverage back to 1993.

Individual Court of Appeals websites have recent opinions, in most instances going back to about 1995, but with rudimentary searching options. District and bankruptcy courts are also represented on the Internet, but most of these sites focus on local rules and procedures rather than the text of decisions. Some require login to the PACER case management system for access to opinions and have no full-text search capabilities. The U.S. Courts website's Court Locator (www.uscourts.gov/court-locator) has a page with links to all court websites grouped by state.

§ 3–3. State Court Cases

Although federal law governs an increasing range of activities, state courts have a vital lawmaking role in many important areas such as family law, contracts, insurance, and substantive criminal law. A state's court of last resort has the final say in interpreting the state's constitution and statutes.

The structure of most state court systems roughly follows the federal paradigm, with trial courts, intermediate appellate courts, and a court of last resort. Be aware, however, that a few states have no intermediate appellate courts, with appeals going directly from the trial court to the state supreme court. Other states have more complicated systems; Oklahoma and Texas, for example, have separate courts of last resort for civil and criminal matters.

A good way to develop a quick familiarity with a state court system is to examine a chart of its structure, indicating the jurisdiction of the various courts and the routes of appeal within the court hierarchy. The National Center for State Courts' Court Statistics Project (www.courtstatistics.org) has a map linking to the chart for each individual state. More detailed information can usually be found on a state court system's website.

Just as Supreme Court decisions are published both in the official *U.S. Reports* and in commercial reporters, decisions from state appellate courts are traditionally published both in official reports, issued by or under the auspices of the courts themselves, and in West's series of National Reporter System volumes.

Westlaw and Lexis are virtually comprehensive sources for state court decisions. They include some opinions not available in print, but coverage is generally limited to the same courts for which reports are published. Relatively few state trial court decisions are available either in print or online, although Westlaw does have Trial Court Orders collections with selected recent decisions from most states. In a global search from the main Westlaw screen, you may need to filter by both Cases and Trial Court Orders to find all relevant judicial decisions.

National Reporter System. West's National Reporter System includes a series of *regional reporters* publishing the decisions of the appellate courts of the fifty states and the District of Columbia. The National Reporter System divides the country into seven regions, and publishes the decisions of the appellate courts of the states in each region together. Cases may be found online but they are still cited to these reporters, so it's worth understanding their content. The reporters, the citations for their current series, and the states they cover are:

Atlantic Reporter (A.3d): Connecticut, Delaware, the District of Columbia, Maine, Maryland, New Hampshire, New Jersey, Pennsylvania, Rhode Island, Vermont

North Eastern Reporter (N.E.3d): Illinois, Indiana, Massachusetts, New York, Ohio

North Western Reporter (N.W.2d): Iowa, Michigan, Minnesota, Nebraska, North Dakota, South Dakota, Wisconsin

Pacific Reporter (P.3d): Alaska, Arizona, California, Colorado, Hawai'i, Idaho, Kansas, Montana, Nevada, New Mexico, Oklahoma, Oregon, Utah, Washington, Wyoming

South Eastern Reporter (S.E.2d): Georgia, North Carolina, South Carolina, Virginia, West Virginia

South Western Reporter (S.W.3d): Arkansas, Kentucky, Missouri, Tennessee, Texas

Southern Reporter (So.3d): Alabama, Florida, Louisiana, Mississippi

These sets are supplemented by separate reporters for two of the most populous states, *California Reporter* (Cal. Rptr. 3d) and *New York Supplement* (N.Y.S.3d). (Cases from the highest courts of California and New York appear in both the regional and the state reporter, while lower court cases are not published in the *Pacific* or *North Eastern Reporter*.)

In most states, cases appear in both official and regional reporter editions. The citation manuals require parallel citations to both sources *only* for cases cited in documents submitted to that state's courts. In other documents such as law review articles and memoranda, only the National Reporter System citation is used. If citing to a regional reporter, remember to identify the deciding court in parentheses with the date.

If you have a citation to only one report of a case, there are several ways to find its parallel citation. The simplest is usually to retrieve the case in an online service, which will generally provide both citations. Remember that not all cases have parallel citations. Only the official reports exist for cases decided before West created the National Reporter System in the 1880s; and the West reporter citation may be the only citation for recent cases in states that have discontinued their official reports and have not instituted public domain citation systems.

As it does with cases in its federal court reports, Westlaw has page images of cases in regional reporters back to the beginning of the National Reporter System. In most instances, the services all include star paging references to both regional and official versions.

Official Reports. Like the *U.S. Reports*, state official reports are the authoritative version of a court's decisions and must be cited in briefs before that court. Twenty-five states, however, have ceased publishing official reports series and have designated an online version or a West reporter as the authoritative source of state case law.

For cases before the beginning of the National Reporter System in the 1880s, the official state reports are the only and authoritative source. Page images of these early volumes are available digitally in HeinOnline's State Reports: A Historical Archive and from LLMC Digital (www.llmcdigital.org).

As with the early *U.S. Reports* volumes, the early reports of several of the older states were once cited as nominative reports (identified by the names of their reporters). Many of these volumes have now been incorporated into the numbered series, but you may still need to use an abbreviations dictionary or other reference work to understand some case citations. The online services generally recognize nominative reporter citations, so you may not need to decipher the abbreviation in order to retrieve a case.

Other Sources. In addition to Westlaw and Lexis, other online services also have state court decisions.

Bloomberg Law coverage extends back well into the 19th century, and others generally have coverage back to the mid-20th century or earlier. Google Scholar has free state appellate court opinions back to at least 1950, with the options to search a specific state or all state jurisdictions.

Court websites generally have decisions beginning in the mid- to late-1990s, but the scope of coverage can vary widely. A few state supreme courts have complete retrospective coverage of their opinions, while others are limited to only the most recent slip opinions.

Decisions from Indian tribal courts can be difficult to find. VersusLaw (www.versuslaw.com) has the most thorough online coverage, with free access to its material available through the Tribal Court Clearinghouse (www.tribal-institute.org). *West's American Tribal Law Reporter* (available on Westlaw to some subscribers) has coverage back to 1997 of decisions from more than twenty tribal courts. Other sources are described in a guide from the University of Washington, Tribal Court Decisions: Sources (lib.law.washington.edu/content/guides/TribalCt).

§ 3–4. Online Keyword Research

Chapter 1 provided a brief overview of basic online research techniques that can be applied in any service. This section focuses more specifically on ways to find cases effectively. It begins with a discussion of Westlaw and Lexis resources, but for researchers without access to these services alternatives are available. Subscription and free resources cover a great deal of case law, with a range of search capabilities. These other services, however, generally lack the synopses, headnotes, and other editorial materials that Westlaw and Lexis add to make cases easier to understand and to connect them topically to related sources.

a. Westlaw

As noted in Chapter 1, Westlaw permits you to run a search from the main screen without first selecting a particular type of materials, such as cases. After searching, you can filter the results to view just the cases and then apply additional filters for jurisdiction, topic, and date. Choosing at the outset to search only cases, however, allows you to take greater advantage of some of the more powerful research tools Westlaw offers.

In online case research, you first choose whether or not to limit a search to a specific jurisdiction. For some issues, it may not matter what courts in other states have decided. The only relevant cases are those from a particular state or within a narrow doctrinal area. For other research questions, however, cases from other jurisdictions can be persuasive authority or may provide useful analogies.

Westlaw can find cases from every federal and state jurisdiction with one search, but for most research questions your best approach is to focus first on decisions from a specific state. You can either filter global results to display cases from one state, or choose that state's cases at the outset. Because federal courts often are required to interpret state laws, sometimes involving issues that have not yet arisen in the state courts, you should usually search cases from both the state courts and the relevant federal jurisdictions (the U.S. Supreme Court, the particular U.S. Court of Appeals, and the U.S. District Courts within the state). This is done in Westlaw by checking the "Include Related Federal" box on the Jurisdiction screen. If you search both state and federal cases, you can filter by jurisdiction to read the state cases first.

Westlaw's WestSearch technology allows you to create a simple, plain-language search, much as you would in Google or another search engine. It finds cases based on the words you use as well as other factors such as alternate terms and usage patterns by other researchers. This can be an excellent way to find a few relevant cases. Case research, however, is not like a general Internet search because you need to make sure that you are finding not just some cases but all relevant cases. Using Westlaw's more power-ful search features such as proximity connectors, truncation, and document fields will help you do this.

The most effective Westlaw searches take advantage of the editorial synopsis and headnotes that precede each case. This focuses retrieval to cases that turn on the specific research issues, rather than any and all cases that mention the search terms.

Westlaw treats the synopsis and headnotes as fields to which a search can be restricted. Limiting a Westlaw search to cases and then clicking on "Advanced Search" shows a long list of case document fields, including the introductory *Synopsis* and the

Digest containing the numbered headnotes. While each of these fields can be searched separately, often the strongest search is one that encompasses the synopsis and digest by using both fields at once (*Synopsis/Digest*). A search for *vicious /3 dog* in the Synopsis and Digest fields will retrieve a smaller body of cases more precisely on point than a simple full-text search for *vicious /3 dog*.

Field searches can also be conducted by using two-letter abbreviations on the main search screen. Entering *SY,DI(vicious /3 dog)* is a shortcut that automatically focuses a search on cases, because other documents such as statutes and secondary sources don't have these fields, and leads very quickly to the most relevant decisions.

The Synopsis and Digest fields are powerful tools for finding the most relevant cases, but for comprehensive research they must be supplemented by full-text keyword searches or other approaches. Westlaw has cases for which it does not provide editorial material, including many unreported decisions. Because these cases have no synopses or headnotes, a search limited to these fields would miss them entirely.

Searches can also be restricted to other fields of the case document, including the names of the parties (*Party Name* or *TI*) and the judge writing the opinion (*Judge* or *JU*). The easiest way to use these fields in Westlaw is to enter terms on the Advanced Search screen, but remember that these fields are listed only if your search is limited to case law.

Once a search is entered, Westlaw displays a list of cases, with a snapshot view of where the search terms appear. Some cases have a red or yellow flag to the left of their names, indicating that they may no longer be good law (although you need to read the citing case to determine the significance of a flag). When displayed in full, each case is accompanied by tabs at the top linking to briefs and other filings, negative treatment, case history, and citing references.

The negative treatment and case history tabs are vital to determining the current validity of the case, but the citing references serve a broader purpose in case research. They are another way to broaden retrieval beyond the cases that match your keywords. A decision may not use your search terms, but if it cites a case you already know to be relevant it may address the issues you are researching. The other cases it cites may then lead you to new research avenues. This process of using citing references and verifying that the cases you have found are "good law" are discussed later in the chapter, in § 3–7 beginning on page 91.

b. Lexis

Lexis is a leading resource for case law because it has comprehensive coverage and includes editorial material that can help focus a search. Cases on Lexis have Case Summaries and headnotes, accompanied by computer-generated "core terms" listing major keywords found in the opinion.

A Lexis Case Summary consists of three parts: Procedural Posture, explaining the nature and status of the litigation; Overview, summarizing the facts of the case; and Outcome, providing a brief description of the court's decision. An advanced search can be restricted to the *Summary* segment to find those cases most likely to be on point.

Lexis, like Westlaw, allows you to do a global search across all sources and then filter your results to find cases. It also gives you the option of searching its full collection of case law or limiting a search to decisions from a particular jurisdiction, with the option to include related federal content.

You can also click on the "Browse Topics" link at the top of the Lexis screen to use the classification system applied to headnotes. Once on the screen listing the outline of topics, you can search for keywords in the topic headings to find summaries of relevant cases and links to the full text.

Lexis headnotes are accompanied by headings showing how they fit into more general legal doctrines. Clicking on one of these headings and then "Get Documents" leads to a list of other cases assigned to the same topic.

The Lexis case display shows a summary of subsequent case treatment, including the number of citing decisions and other documents. These Shepard's references are vital in determining the validity of your case and in expanding your research, and will be discussed with other citators in § 3–7.

c. *Bloomberg Law and Other Resources*

Bloomberg Law has a nearly comprehensive collection of federal and state case law, but for most cases it lacks editorial summaries such as introductory synopses or headnotes to provide research springboards to other cases. It does include headnotes for cases published in BNA's series of topical reporters in specialized areas such as communications, employment law, environmental law, intellectual property, and trade. In a case with BNA headnotes, you can click on the classification number in a headnote to find other cases on similar issues.

Lower-cost services such as Casemaker, Fastcase, and VersusLaw also include broad coverage of case law. They offer a variety of sophisticated search approaches, with features such as truncation, Boolean connectors, document fields, and plain-language searching. These services, like Bloomberg Law, have the full, searchable text of court opinions, but they generally have no introductory summaries or headnotes to provide springboards for further research. For many lawyers, access to either Casemaker or Fastcase is a benefit of bar membership.

Free access to case law is available from Google Scholar (scholar.google.com), which has coverage of federal cases since 1923 and state appellate cases since at least 1950. The way to access these cases is to choose "Case law" on the main screen; you can then specify the court or courts you wish to search. Results can be sorted by relevance or date. A "How cited" link shows excerpts from later decisions citing the displayed case and lists all citing documents.

Innovative online approaches to case research are also available. Ravel (www.ravellaw.com) presents not just search results but also an interactive map of circles showing how the most significant cases are linked together, with circle size indicating the importance of each case and lines connecting each case to the cases it cites and those that cite it.

Websites for individual courts or jurisdictions also offer opinions, but some sites are much more accessible and comprehensive than others. Some state court sites simply provide chronological access to opinions with no full-text searching, while others have searchable retrospective collections of appellate court decisions. With the exception of a very few exemplary sites, court websites are not the best place to do case research but can be useful for obtaining copies of new decisions and monitoring developments.

§ 3–5.   Key Number Research

West editors write headnotes for each case and assign each headnote to a classification indicating its specific legal issue. This classification plan, known as the *key number system*, consists of almost 400 topics, arranged alphabetically from Abandoned and Lost Property to Zoning and Planning. Each topic is then divided into key numbers designating specific points of law. This classification system serves the same purpose for legal topics that call numbers do for library books, in that it allows related items to be classed together whether or not they use the same keywords. Similar legal issues may arise, for example, in cases involving dogs and other animals, but it may not occur to you to search for both *cat* and *horse* as well as *dog*.

These key numbers are important tools for finding cases, on Westlaw or in printed volumes of digests. By using key numbers, you can frequently find relevant cases that a keyword search would miss.

a. Using Key Numbers on Westlaw

On Westlaw, you can search for relevant key numbers or use the numbers assigned to one case's headnotes as springboards to further cases. For use in Westlaw, each of the topics has been assigned a number. *Animals* is topic 28, for example, and cases on dog bites are classed under Animals key number 66.5, so this issue is identified as *28k66.5*.

The simplest way to incorporate key numbers into your case research is to note which cases you find through keyword searches or other methods have particularly relevant headnotes, and then use their headnotes to find other cases. You do this by clicking on a headnote's hyperlinked key number, which leads you to a list of other cases under this number. You can then search within these results for cases that meet your specific facts or legal issues.

Any time a global search is run on Westlaw, the results show not only cases, statutes, secondary sources, and other documents, but a list of the ten most relevant key numbers. Some of these may not be related at all to your research, but others may indeed be of value. If so, you can click on the link to retrieve case headnotes classified to the key number. You can limit results to a specific jurisdiction or search within the headnotes for specific keywords, and click from the headnotes to the full text of the cases.

You can also click on Tools and then West Key Number System to see the entire range of classifications. From this screen you can browse appropriate topics or search for terms appearing in key number descriptions. An advantage of this method is that it gives you the context of the individual key numbers at the outset; reading through the outline may help clarify issues or raise concerns you had not yet considered. In most instances, however, a pinpoint reference from a case or keyword search is a faster and more reliable starting point.

Finally, you can use topics and key numbers in combination with other terms to create a very precise and effective search. Adding *TO(28)* or *TO(animals)* to a search focuses retrieval on animal-related cases, and including the term *28k66.5* immediately restricts your search to bite cases. Obviously you are not going to begin a research project with a search like *28k66.5*, but once you are familiar with the key numbers you can use them to craft very refined searches.

b. West Digests

West topics and key numbers can also be used in print series of volumes known as *digests*. These are tools that reprint the headnote summaries by key number, serving as a subject index to case law.

West digests are published for the entire country and for specific jurisdictions. State digests include references to cases from the state's courts and to federal cases arising from the U.S. District Courts in that state. Federal court decisions are covered in *West's Federal Practice Digest 5th*, with coverage beginning in 2003, which is gradually replacing *Federal Practice Digest 4th*, covering cases since the mid-1980s. Cases from both federal and state courts can be found in a series known as *Decennial Digests* (so called because each series originally covered ten years), updated by *General Digest* volumes collecting headnotes from all West reporters and published every few weeks.

West reprints headnotes in which courts define or interpret legally significant terms in a separate multivolume set, *Words and Phrases*, arranged alphabetically rather than by key number. This can be a useful tool when the meaning of a specific term is at issue. Headnotes with judicial definitions can also be found on Westlaw by searching the *Words & Phrases* or *WP* field.

The simplest way to approach a digest is to use the headnotes of a case known to be on point as a springboard, but you can also begin your research in a Descriptive-Word Index shelved at the beginning or the end of a digest set. This index lists thousands of factual and legal terms, with references to key numbers. You can also go directly to the digest topic that appears most relevant to a problem and analyze its outline to select the appropriate key number for a specific issue. As with the online Key Number

System, this method may suggest new avenues of research but is usually more time-consuming than starting in the index.

The key number system has been in use for more than a century, but the law of course has not remained static in that time. Old doctrines have faded in significance and new areas of law have developed. West attempts to reflect changes by revising and expanding old topics and by establishing new topics. When new or revised topics are introduced, West editors reclassify the headnotes in thousands of older cases. On Westlaw, the numbers assigned to older cases are updated when the key number system is revised, and the current classification can be used to find relevant cases of any age. The new classifications are also used when state or federal digest volumes are recompiled. New or revised topics are accompanied by tables for converting older topics and key numbers to those newly adopted, and vice versa. These may come in handy if a reference found in an older case or an index can no longer be found.

It may take several years for new areas of legal doctrine to be recognized and to receive adequate coverage. It took five years of sex discrimination cases, for example, before their headnotes were classed under a new key number for "Employment practices—Sex discrimination" instead of the broad "Nature of rights protected by civil rights laws." Because cases in newly developing areas of the law are often assigned to general key numbers, key number research is usually not the easiest way to find cases in these areas.

The West Key Number System, online or in print, is the most comprehensive subject guide to American case law. Be aware, however, that headnotes may reflect dicta and that digest entries generally don't indicate whether a case is still good law. A textual discussion of an area of law, such as in a treatise or a law review article, usually offers a clearer and more selective introduction to relevant case law.

§ 3–6.   *American Law Reports* Annotations

Several publishers in the late 19th century selected "leading cases" for publication, with commentaries, or *annotations*, that described other decisions on similar issues. The annotations proved to be valuable research tools and are still being used.

The modern successor to these early annotated reporters is *American Law Reports* (*ALR*), which is now published as *ALR7th* for general and state legal issues, and *ALR Federal 3d* for issues of federal law. (Another series, *ALR International*, focuses on treatment of international law issues by U.S. and foreign courts, and will be discussed in Chapter 9.)

ALR annotations are available on both Westlaw and Lexis. In either Westlaw or Lexis, a general search in secondary sources can quickly be filtered to highlight *ALR* results.

Annotations summarize the cases on a specific topic and classify decisions that have reached similar and conflicting results. An *ALR* annotation directly on point can save you considerable research time. It does the initial time-consuming work of finding relevant cases and arranging them according to specific fact patterns and holdings.

Annotations differ significantly from other narrative resources such as treatises and law review articles. Their purpose is to systematically present the varied judicial decisions from around the country, not to criticize these decisions or to integrate case law into broader concerns. Each *ALR* annotation includes a detailed subject index, a table listing the jurisdictions of the cases discussed, and leads to related annotations, encyclopedias, and other sources. They are research tools rather than secondary authority that might persuade a tribunal. If they are cited, it is as convenient compilations of prevailing judicial doctrine.

The online versions of *ALR* annotations can be found through keyword searches, just like cases or law review articles. Because annotations describe the facts of the cases discussed, including aspects other than the subject of the annotation, a full-text search may turn up numerous documents on unrelated topics. It is often best to limit a Westlaw search to the *title* portion of the document by using the *TI* field or the Advanced Search screen. Relevance ranking should also ensure that the most useful annotations appear early in a list of search results.

The basic tool for subject access to the printed version of *ALR* is the nine-volume *ALR Index* (also available on Westlaw). A less comprehensive *ALR Quick Index* covers only *ALR3d* to *7th*, and a separate *ALR Federal Quick Index* is limited to *ALR Fed* to *ALR Fed 3d* annotations.

No matter when an annotation was originally published, annual supplements provide references to more recent cases. If the law on a subject covered by an annotation changes substantially, a new annotation may supersede the older one. The older volume's pocket part or other supplement alerts you to the existence of the newer treatment; online, a notice and a link to the newer annotation replace the older work. Superseding annotations are also listed in an "Annotation History Table" in the back of each volume of the *ALR Index*.

Remember that *ALR* annotations include a list of other annotations on related topics. If at first you don't find an annotation directly on point but see one on a similar issue, the most productive next step may be to turn to that annotation and read through its list of related annotations. This list could lead to analogies or concepts you may not have considered in your initial search.

You can also use a case or statute to find relevant annotations. Westlaw includes coverage of annotations as citing references, and many annotated codes and encyclopedias provide references to relevant *ALR* annotations.

Annotations can be very useful research tools for many legal problems. If an annotation has been written on a point being researched, that means someone has already examined the issue and collected almost every relevant case. Because each annotation is written about a specific topic, however, coverage in the series is not comprehensive or encyclopedic. There are many issues for which no annotation can be found.

§ 3–7. Citators

Under the doctrine of precedent, the holdings of governing cases determine the resolution of issues in subsequent controversies. A precedential decision continues to have binding effect regardless of its age, but its authority can change either suddenly or through gradual erosion. A decision might be reversed on appeal to a higher court or overruled years later by a decision of the same court. Later cases may also criticize or question the reasoning of a decision, or limit its holding to a specific factual situation. Any of these circumstances can negate or diminish the authority of a case.

Before relying on any case, you must verify its current validity. This process of updating cases was traditionally performed by checking printed volumes known as *Shepard's Citations*, and as a result it is sometimes known as *Shepardizing*. Shepard's information is now available electronically on Lexis, and other services have citators with similar features.

Citators perform three major functions:

• Case history: References to other proceedings in the same case, allowing you to trace its judicial history;

• Case validity: Indications of subsequent cases that have overruled, limited, or otherwise diminished a case's precedential value, providing the information you need to determine whether it remains "good law"; and

• Citing references: Research leads to later citing cases, as well as periodical articles, *ALR* annotations, and other resources, enabling you to find related cases and to trace the development of a legal doctrine forward from a known case to the present.

The major services incorporate citator information into their case display. Symbols or flags next to case names highlight significant citations. Westlaw has tabs at the top of the case display, while Lexis and Bloomberg Law have links to the right of the case showing the number of citing documents by the nature of their analysis.

Case History. Seeing other decisions in the same litigation allows you to follow the proceeding through the court system, to clarify facts, and to determine if your case has been affirmed or reversed on appeal. Westlaw uses a History tab at the top of the case, while Lexis and Bloomberg Law indicate to the right of the screen that there are case history documents. Be aware, however, that only decisions also available on the service are listed. Every service has numerous cases with no indication of what happened before or after the decision, because no other opinions in the litigation are online.

Case Validity. Symbols next to case names serve as notices about their validity. Red flags or stop signs indicate that a case's precedential value has been seriously affected. In Westlaw, a blue striped flag indicates that a federal case is currently on appeal. Other symbols, such as yellow flags or caution symbols, indicate that a holding may have been questioned or distinguished in subsequent cases. Clicking on this symbol, or on a link to the right of the case display, takes you to a list of the more recent decisions.

In addition to the flags or symbols, Westlaw has a "Negative Treatment" tab at the top of the case display while Lexis and Bloomberg Law include tables to the right of case displays listing analysis symbols such as "Caution" or "Distinguished" and the number of citing cases for each.

These signals and symbols are just tools for your use, not authoritative statements of the law. Relying on a red flag or a stop sign is no substitute for reading a citing document and determining for yourself its scope and effect. A case that has been overruled on one point may still be good law on other issues, but learning this requires reading the overruling case itself and perhaps examining *its* subsequent history.

Be aware that terms such as "negative" are broadly defined. A lower court decision that declines to extend a Supreme Court precedent beyond its intended scope is listed as "distinguishing" its holding. This is considered negative treatment, even though it has no impact on the Supreme Court decision's precedent.

Citing References. Citators are invaluable resources not only because they ensure the validity of the cases you've found. They also serve as powerful links from one case to others addressing similar issues, providing one of the most effective ways to find sources for further research. You can use citators to shape your research and to focus in on specific aspects of relevant cases. Even the absence of citing references can provide important information about a case; if a decision has remained uncited for decades, it may indicate that it is a neglected backwater that might not be accorded much weight by a current court.

The citing references can be limited in various ways, by document type, headnote number, jurisdiction, or keyword. *Search Within Results* on Westlaw or Lexis can focus immediately on those documents applying a precedent to a particular set of facts. Westlaw and Lexis also sort citing decisions by the extent to which they discuss the cited case, so that you can focus quickly on what are likely to be the most relevant and informative decisions.

Another way to find citing references on a specific point of law in Westlaw or Lexis is to use the headnotes in the case display to pinpoint a legal issue and then click on the "Cases that cite this headnote" or "Shepardize—Narrow by this Headnote" link. This should take you immediately to the most relevant cases. Lexis also has a "Legal Issue Trail" feature that allows you to select a specific passage in an opinion and retrieve a list of more recent cases that cite the opinion on that point of law.

All three services also offer alert services that can monitor developments in a case's history or citing references and send you e-mail notices of new citing references. In Westlaw and Lexis, alerts can be tailored for references meeting specific criteria such as cited headnote number or jurisdiction.

Other research services also have citators. Casemaker's Casecheck and Fastcase's Authority Check provide links to subsequent citing cases, but without codes or flags indicating the nature of the citations. A Google Scholar case display includes a "How cited" link that lists citing cases and provides excerpts from these cases. It does not, however, indicate whether a case has been overruled or otherwise limited.

Although their editorial treatment and formats differ, citators generally provide coverage of the same citing cases. Coverage of secondary sources, however, varies dramatically depending on what materials are available from the online service. Westlaw and Lexis have the largest collections of law review articles, and these are included in their citator results. Westlaw also includes *ALR* annotations and Thomson Reuters treatises, while Shepard's has treatises and encyclopedias published by LexisNexis or Matthew Bender. These references can be enormously helpful in putting your case in a broader context and leading you to other relevant primary authority.

CHAPTER 4

STATUTES AND CONSTITUTIONS

Images of some resources discussed in this chapter are at **libguides.law.virginia.edu/nutshell12/ch4**

---

§ 4–1. Introduction

The preceding chapter focused on case law because of the importance of appellate decisions in the common law system and in American legal education. Legislative enactments, however, play just as vital a role as decisions in today's legal system. Most appellate court decisions, in fact, involve the application or interpretation of statutes rather than the consideration of common law principles.

This chapter considers both legislation and constitutions, which establish the form and limitations of government power. Statutes and constitutions are often published together, and similar methods are used to research both sources. In considering statutes or constitutional provisions, it is important to find not only the relevant text but also cases that interpret this text and define its terms. The most important research sources for both statutes and constitutions are *annotated codes*, which provide the text of laws in force accompanied by notes of court decisions.

It is important to determine early in the research process whether a problem involves statutory or constitutional provisions, and whether these issues are matters of federal or state law. Substantive criminal law, for example, is generally defined by the enactments of a state legislature, while defendants' procedural rights are determined by both federal and state constitutional law. As legislatures enact statutes to govern traditional common law areas such as contract and tort, more and more questions involve statutory research. Secondary sources and cases generally provide references to the relevant provisions, so it should soon become apparent from your introductory research whether statutory research is warranted.

§ 4–2.   Publication of Statutes

American statutes are published in three basic stages, in either print or electronic form. The first version of a newly enacted statute is the *slip law*, which is issued by itself on a single sheet or as a pamphlet with separate pagination. Legislative websites and subscription services generally provide convenient access to the texts of new acts. (Instead of slip laws, some websites have only *enrolled bills*, which are the final versions of bills as they were passed by the legislature and presented to the executive for approval.)

Next are the *session laws*. The acts are arranged by date of passage and published in separate volumes for each legislative term. In most jurisdictions, the session laws constitute the authoritative, binding text of the laws (*positive law*). Codes and other forms are only *prima facie* evidence of statutory language. This means that the session law controls, unless the legislature has enacted the code as positive law.

Session laws have limited value as research tools. Researchers usually need the laws currently in force, rather than the acts passed during a specific legislative term. They also need convenient access to amendments and related legislation. For this they turn to the third form of statutory publication, the *statutory compilation* or *code*.

Codes collect current statutes of general and permanent application and arrange them by subject. The statutes are grouped into broad subject topics, usually called *titles*, and within each title they are divided into chapters and then numbered sections. The sections of an act may be codified together or may be scattered by subject through several different titles.

Some jurisdictions have official code publications containing the text of the statutes in force. If an official edition is published, it is usually the authoritative text and should be cited in briefs and pleadings. Every jurisdiction provides free online access to the text of its code, usually through the legislature's website, but some sites include warnings that the online version is unofficial and that only the printed volumes have the official text.

Most official codes, in print or online, are *unannotated*; that is, they do not include references to judicial decisions that have applied or construed the statutes. That is why *annotated codes* with summaries of these decisions are the most useful resources for statutory research. Some statutory sections have been interpreted in thousands of court cases, and are accompanied in annotated codes by copious notes arranged by subject. Other sections may have no annotations at all, if they are uncontroversial and have not led to litigation or are too new to have been considered in any published court decisions.

Because most annotated codes are commercial publications, they are generally not available online at free Internet sites. Westlaw and Lexis have annotated codes for federal law and for all fifty states. These services are among the most thorough and up-to-date resources for statutory research, incorporating new legislation within days of enactment and providing a variety of research links from a code section to related cases and secondary sources.

Remember that annotated codes are usually not authoritative sources of the text of statutes. Most are unofficial commercial publications, and the official code is controlling if there is any discrepancy between it and an annotated code.

§ 4–3. Statutory Research

Statutory research is one area where online resources have not wholly supplanted print. Even experienced researchers who do most of their work online find that printed code volumes can be of value in statutory research. Print can make it easier to find related provisions and to place a section in its context. Statutory provisions often have multiple subsections and sub-subsections, and you need to understand how these different subsections relate to each other. You also need to see an entire code chapter or title in order to understand the context and purpose of an individual section. Skimming through a few pages in a code volume can be easier than going from document to document in an online service. In addition, the vague and technical wording of statutes means that online keyword searches are often less productive than using the indexes that accompany annotated codes. We nonetheless begin our discussion with online resources, the most common starting points for statutory research.

a. Online Codes

This discussion of research procedures focuses primarily on Westlaw and Lexis, which have highly useful annotated versions of codes and the same search technique for statutes from all jurisdictions. Search approaches and features in other online resources for statutes may vary from state to state.

Online annotated codes are complex resources that can be difficult to search successfully. A full-text search finds words appearing either in the statutes themselves or in the annotations of cases, and may retrieve far too many irrelevant documents. Your best approach is often to focus a search on the statutory language and exclude the notes of decisions. The *Statutory Text* (or *TE*) field on Westlaw contains the headings, the text, and any official notes, but not the annotations. You can also search just the words used to identify a title and the section, often a quick way to find the most relevant sections. Westlaw uses the *Preliminary* (or *PR*) field for title, subtitle and chapter designations, and *Caption* (or *CA*) for the section number and description. These segments on Lexis are called Heading and Section, respectively.

Be aware that Westlaw and Lexis treat each code section as a separate document, and a search retrieves only those specific *sections* that match the particular query. Because it is essential in statutory research to understand the context of a specific provision, you should examine nearby sections after finding one that is on point. There are several ways to do this.

Both Westlaw and Lexis allow you to click on left and right arrows to browse the sections immediately preceding and following the document on your screen. A more comprehensive way to grasp the context of a section is to see the table of contents for its chapter by clicking on the hyperlinked heading at the top of the display. By scanning the list of sections, you may find others (perhaps labeled "Definitions" or "Exclusions") that have a very direct impact on your research.

Other services generally offer fewer options and features than do Westlaw or Lexis. Subscription sites such as Bloomberg Law offer sophisticated search options but no case annotations. Most free websites do not include any annotations, and many have fairly simple options for keyword searching. They may nonetheless offer convenient and current access to the statutory text. No matter what site you use, it is vital to make sure that your source is up to date and to browse nearby sections to make sure that important definitions or cross-references are not missed.

b. Citators

Finding relevant code sections is just the first step of statutory research. Before relying on a statute as authority, you must verify that it is still in force and ascertain how it has been affected by subsequent legislation and by judicial decisions.

Annotated codes are indispensable because they provide regularly updated information on a statute's validity and treatment. Even the annotated codes, however, lack the most recent legislative changes and references to *all* citing decisions. It can take weeks or months for amendments to be incorporated into the code database, and even longer for case annotations to be written and assigned to specific code sections. Much more current research leads can be found on Westlaw or Lexis.

Westlaw's coverage of statutes under the "Citing References" tab expands greatly on the cases summarized in code annotations. It lists the most recent court decisions and other citing cases. For each opinion, a brief section of text shows the context in which the code section is cited. Westlaw also displays recent and pending legislation, and scholarly articles, encyclopedias, and treatises that cite the statute. You can narrow a citing references display by document type, jurisdiction, specific keywords, and other criteria.

Statutes on Westlaw include signals based on this information. A red flag appears at the top of the display if a code section has been found invalid or unconstitutional, or if it has been amended by recent legislation not yet incorporated into the text. A yellow flag shows that a section's validity has been called into doubt, or that pending legislation would amend a section if enacted.

The Lexis display of code sections does not include flags indicating unconstitutionality or recent amendments, but clicking on the "Shepardize" link provides this information. You can then narrow results by particular citing treatment, jurisdiction, or keywords.

A useful Lexis feature is that you can restrict a listing to cases and other documents that cite a specific subsection of a statute. You do this by clicking on the "Subsection reports by specific court citation" link, leading to a listing of the exact references courts have used for statutory provisions. This way, you can home in immediately on the three or four cases citing subsection (b)(2)(A) without having to sort through hundreds of other cases citing the section as a whole or other subsections. Many code sections have numerous subsections and sub-subsections, and this can be an invaluable time-saver.

c. *Indexes and Tables*

Even if you normally do all of your other work online, you might find it easier to begin statutory research with a printed code. Many statutes are written in a technical language designed to reduce ambiguities in interpretation, and the terminology used may not be the words that would occur to you in creating an online search. A code's plain-language subject index can often lead more quickly to relevant provisions and may reveal related sections that you would otherwise miss.

Indexes. Code indexes are lengthy documents filled with cross-references and long lists of subheadings. If you look under "Birds," for example, you may find nothing but an entry such as "See Migratory birds" or "Migratory birds, this index." These cross-references and other leads may seem a little tedious to follow at first, but an index may make it much easier to find statutes than full-text keyword searches that yield too many irrelevant results.

Westlaw has online versions of the indexes that accompany West's printed codes, in the "Tools & Resources" list on the statutes search screen for a specific jurisdiction.

Popular Name Tables. At times you may have a reference to a particular law by its name, without a citation, and need to find the text of the statute. How do you find the Civil Rights Act of 1964? You could look in a subject index under "Civil rights," but it is quicker to use a *popular name table*, which lists acts by name and provides references to citations in the session laws and code. These are available in most printed codes, and Westlaw includes them in its "Tools & Resources" for each jurisdiction.

Popular name tables cover the names by which acts are designated by Congress and state legislatures, but they don't always include the terms by which laws are commonly known. "Title VII" is familiar shorthand for part of the Civil Rights Act of 1964, but the term doesn't appear in the table. In order to find a citation for such a reference, the first step is to find more of the name. It may be simplest to search law reviews for the phrase and then check the footnotes to identify the act and its citation.

Parallel Reference Tables and Parenthetical Notes. At times you may have a citation to a statute that does not take you directly to its place in a code. Some references are to session laws, while others are to outdated codifications. In either instance you will need to determine whether a law is currently in force and, if so, where it is codified. For this, most codes include *parallel reference tables* providing cross-references to the current code sections. Most of these tables also indicate which sections of session laws have been repealed or were of a temporary nature.

Just as parallel reference tables link session laws or older code citations to current code provisions, the parenthetical notes that follow the text of a code section allow you to reconstruct the language of a statute at any given point in the past. Older laws are needed to determine the law in effect and the meaning of terms when instruments such as wills or deeds were drafted. The parenthetical notes provide leads to earlier codifications and to session laws that have amended the section. These references are also the keys to finding legislative history information for a particular enactment.

Some codes make it easier to reconstruct past versions of a statute by indicating the exact changes made. Others merely present a list of citations, and you will need to check the session laws to see what changed. Some codes indicate only recent changes or (particularly in the case of many free Internet sites) have no notes at all.

Westlaw and Lexis have archived versions of state codes for recent years, and reconstructing the law as of a date in the past few decades may simply require a search in the appropriate archive database. For some jurisdictions, including federal law back to 1996, Westlaw's "History" tab includes a Versions feature that shows you older versions and the specific dates when they were in force.

§ 4–4.   Sources for Federal Statutes

The United States Congress meets in two-year terms, consisting of two annual sessions, and enacts several hundred statutes each term. These statutes range from simple designations of commemorative days to complex environmental or tax legislation spanning hundreds of pages. Each act is designated as either a *public law* or a *private law*, and assigned a number indicating the order in which it was passed. Pub. L. 115–1, for example, is the first public law passed during the 115th Congress (2017–18). Private laws, passed to meet special needs of an individual or small group, are little used in the modern era and do not become part of the statutory code.

a. Slip Laws and Session Laws

The first official text of a new federal law is the slip law, an individually paginated pamphlet. The Government Printing Office's Federal Digital System (FDsys) (www.gpo.gov/fdsys/) has PDF files of slip laws beginning with the 104th Congress in 1995. For current legislation this is one of the quickest and most effective sources, with new laws appearing online within a few days or weeks of enactment. If the public law is not yet available, you can check the legislative site Congress.gov (www.congress.gov) for the enrolled bill that was passed by both houses and sent to the President.

After the end of each session of Congress, the slip laws are cumulated, corrected, and issued in bound volumes as the official *United States Statutes at Large* for the session. These are cited by volume and page number. The Migratory Bird Treaty Reform Act of 1998, Pub. L. 105–312, 112 Stat. 2956 (1998), for example, begins on page 2956 of volume 112 of the *Statutes at Large*. There is a delay of about two years before *Statutes at Large* volumes are published, but the slip laws on the FDsys website include the *Statutes at Large* pagination within weeks of enactment.

Public laws are also available online from Westlaw. "U.S. Public Laws" has laws from the current Congress; "U.S. Public Laws-Historical" has coverage back to 1973; and "United States Statutes at Large" has retrospective coverage from 1789 to 1972. Acts before 1973 are available as image-based PDFs, and only citations, dates, and summary information are searchable.

HeinOnline has complete retrospective coverage of the *Statutes at Large* in PDF, with the text of all acts back to 1789 searchable by keyword, title, or citation. The Library of Congress provides free access to the first eighteen volumes of the *Statutes at Large*, through 1875, as part of its "A Century of Lawmaking for a New Nation: U.S. Congressional Documents and Debates, 1774–1875" collection (memory.loc.gov/ammem/amlaw/). Only the index is searchable, but acts can be retrieved by citation.

The easiest way to find court decisions citing acts in the *Statutes at Large* is to do a full-text search for

its citation (e.g., "112 stat 2956") in a case law
database. The online citators don't cover citations to
session laws, but the *United States Code Service*
includes case summaries by *Statutes at Large*
citation in one of its "Annotations to Uncodified Laws
and Treaties" volumes.

Although the *Statutes at Large* is not the most
convenient source for federal legislation, its role in
legal research is vital. In most instances it is the
official statement of the law, and it is a necessary
source for determining the specific language
Congress enacted at any given time. This is a key
step in legislative history research, as will be
discussed in Chapter 5.

b. *The* United States Code

The first official subject compilations of federal
legislation were the *Revised Statutes of the United
States* of 1873, and its second edition of 1878.
Congress enacted the first edition of the *Revised
Statutes* as positive law in its entirety, expressly
repealing the original *Statutes at Large* versions of
its contents. It is therefore the authoritative text for
most laws enacted before 1873, and is still needed
occasionally in modern research. The *Revised
Statutes* is online in PDF form from several sources,
including the Library of Congress as part of its
coverage of the *Statutes at Large*.

Although the *Revised Statutes* rapidly became
outdated, no other official compilation was prepared
for almost fifty years. Finally, in 1926, the first
edition of the *United States Code* was published,

arranging the laws by subject into fifty titles. The *U.S. Code* is published in a new edition of about forty volumes every six years, with annual supplements of one or more bound volumes. These supplements are cumulative, so you only need to consult the main set and its latest supplement.

The *U.S. Code* is now arranged in fifty-four subject titles, generally in alphabetical order. Titles are divided into chapters and then into sections, with a continuous sequence of section numbers for each title. Citations to the *Code* indicate the title, section number, and year. 16 U.S.C. § 704 (2012), for example, is part of title 16 (Conservation), chapter 7 (Protection of Migratory Game and Insectivorous Birds). The chapter number does not appear in the citation.

You should keep in mind that not every federal law is published as a section of the *United States Code*. Some laws appear only in the *Statutes at Large*, and others are published as notes following sections of the code. Whether a statute is published as a code section or a note, or is omitted entirely from the *U.S. Code*, has no effect on its validity.

The *U.S. Code* is available free online from several sources. The most important of these sites is the House of Representatives Office of the Law Revision Counsel (uscode.house.gov), which prepares and publishes the *Code*. The House site allows access by title and section number and has several search options. It also provides access to PDF files for entire code titles, incorporating the material in the supplements to the printed edition of the code. This makes them more convenient than the printed code and supplements, but because they do not mirror the published source they cannot be used for citation purposes.

The *Code* is also available as part of FDsys (www.uscode.gov), with annual editions back to 1994. The FDsys site allows individual sections or chapters to be downloaded in PDF.

Another online source for the *U.S. Code* is HeinOnline, which reproduces every printed edition from 1926 through the most recent supplement in searchable PDF. The older editions can be useful for tracking the history of a provision, and may be needed for a citation to a statute that is no longer in force.

The *Statutes at Large* is traditionally the authoritative source of federal legislation, and the *U.S. Code* is *prima facie* evidence of the law. A growing number of *U.S. Code* titles, however, have been reenacted as positive law, and for them the code is the authoritative text. Lists of all code titles, indicating which have been reenacted, appear in the front of each *U.S. Code* volume and on the Law Revision Counsel and FDsys sites.

The *U.S. Code* in print features a number of research aids, including a multivolume general index and several tables. An "Acts Cited by Popular Name" table lists laws alphabetically under either short titles assigned by Congress or popular names by which they have become known, and parallel reference tables provide links from earlier revisions and from the *Statutes at Large* to *U.S. Code* sections. The tables, but not the index, are available on the Office of the Law Revision Counsel's website.

c. Annotated Codes

The *United States Code* is the preferred source for citing federal laws, but two major shortcomings limit its value in research: (1) it is not updated on a very timely basis, and (2) it has no information about court decisions applying or interpreting code sections. These decisions are so important that most researchers rely on one of two commercially published, annotated editions of the code, *United States Code Annotated* (*USCA*), published by Thomson Reuters and available on Westlaw, or *United States Code Service* (*USCS*), published by LexisNexis and available on Lexis. Beyond the text of the law and notes of court decisions, these commercial editions also provide references to legislative history, administrative regulations, and various secondary sources.

Unlike the official *U.S. Code*, which is published in a new edition every six years, *USCA* and *USCS* consist of volumes of varying ages, all updated with annual pocket parts or pamphlet supplements. Replacement volumes are published when supplements get too unwieldy.

You may need to check both *USCA* and *USCS* for thorough research of a particular statute. Each provides selective annotations of court decisions, and a relevant case may be included in one but not the other. *USCA*'s annotations are generally more extensive, but some court decisions appear only in

USCS—which is also the only source for references to administrative decisions.

Bear in mind that notes of decisions do not follow every code section. Many sections of the *U.S. Code* have not been the subject of judicial interpretation. Some are uncontroversial and have not led to litigation, while others may be too new for any reported cases. If there are no annotations, you will need to interpret a section without the assistance of court decisions directly on point.

As noted, both annotated editions of the code are available online (*USCA* on Westlaw and *USCS* on Lexis). The online codes are updated to incorporate changes from the current session of Congress; notes above the heading on Lexis and at the bottom of the Westlaw display indicate the latest public law incorporated. If a section has been amended by a public law too recent to be incorporated, the Westlaw display includes a red flag with a link to the more current legislative action.

§ 4–5.   Sources for State Statutes

State statutes appear in many of the same forms as their federal counterparts, with slip laws, session laws, codes, and annotated codes. Current session laws and codes are available from government websites, and annotated codes are published both electronically and in print.

a. Slip Laws and Session Laws

State slip laws are rarely distributed widely in print, but every state legislature provides Internet access to recently enacted laws. Two easy ways to find legislative websites are to search for "[state] legislature" or to check a site with multistate links such as the National Conference of State Legislatures (www.ncsl.org).

Each state has a session law publication similar to the *U.S. Statutes at Large*, containing the laws enacted at each sitting of its legislature. The names of these publications vary (e.g., *Acts of Alabama, Statutes of California, Laws of Delaware*). In most states the session laws are the authoritative positive law text of the statutes, and you may need them to examine legislative changes or to reconstruct the language in force at a particular date.

Westlaw and Lexis have the texts of new legislation from every state, with older session laws going back to 1991 or earlier. HeinOnline's Session Laws Library provides PDF versions of each state's session laws, with retrospective coverage to the beginning of statehood and beyond to colonial or territorial laws.

b. Codes

All states have subject compilations of their statutes similar to the *U.S. Code*. Some states publish unannotated official codes, regularly revised on an annual or biennial basis.

Every state makes its code available through its state website, although these free online codes vary widely in their currency, official status, and features. Only a handful of free online state codes include annotations of court decisions, but all of the codes can be searched by keyword and browsed through tables of contents. Several convenient compilations of links are available, including lists of state legal materials at the Law Library of Congress (www.loc.gov/law/) and Legal Information Institute (www.law.cornell. edu/states/).

Most researchers rely on annotated codes containing summaries of relevant court decisions and other references, published in most instances by either Thomson Reuters or LexisNexis. Several states have competing codes from both publishers. Westlaw and Lexis have annotated codes from all fifty states, as well as the District of Columbia, Guam, Puerto Rico, and the Virgin Islands.

The outline and arrangement of code material vary from state to state. While most codes are divided into titles and sections, like the *U.S. Code*, several states have individual codes designated by name rather than title number (e.g., California Civil Code, New York Penal Law, or Texas Water Code).

State codes usually have references to the original session laws in parenthetical notes following each section, but only some include notes indicating the changes made by each amendment. Most also include tables with cross references from session law citations and earlier codifications to the current code.

The Bluebook and *ALWD Guide* have listings by state of the names and citations of current official and commercially published codes. State legal research guides (listed in Appendix A) provide information about earlier codes and statutory revisions for individual states.

c. Multistate Research Sources

Most state statutory research requires finding the law in one particular state, and that state's code will be your primary research tool. Sometimes, however, you may want to compare statutory provisions among states or survey legislation throughout the country. Multistate surveys of state laws can be time-consuming, since different state codes do not necessarily use the same terminology for similar issues, but several resources can help to make the job a bit easier.

In either Westlaw or Lexis you can filter a global search to focus on statutes by jurisdiction, and in Westlaw you can opt to search the annotated or unannotated codes of all fifty states. A multistate search can save considerable time, although you should remember that any single search is unlikely to retrieve all relevant laws. You may also need to search individual codes or state code indexes.

Westlaw and Lexis also feature fifty-state surveys linking to state code provisions on various topics. Westlaw's 50 State Statutory Surveys, listed under "Secondary Sources," include several hundred surveys prepared by West editors consisting of an introductory overview followed by links to the state code provisions. A "State by State Analysis" link opens a PDF document with summaries of each state's provisions.

Another source for multistate surveys is Richard A. Leiter, *National Survey of State Laws* (7th ed. 2015, available on HeinOnline). This collection is arranged by topic, and includes charts summarizing statutes on several social and political issues such as gun control, marijuana, prayer in public schools, and the right to die. The tables highlight specific aspects of each state's law, allowing immediate comparisons of these provisions, with citations to the codes for fuller examination.

Free Internet sites provide multistate access to code provisions in some subject areas. One of the most comprehensive sources is the Legal Information Institute's topical index to state statutes (www.law.cornell.edu/wex/state_statutes), with links to code sites in several dozen broad categories. Sites collecting statutes on specific topics are also available, but it is important to verify that any resource you use is regularly and reliably updated.

Topical looseleaf services (see Chapter 8) often collect state laws in their subject areas, making it easy to compare state provisions in areas such as taxation or employment law, and numerous other online and print resources reprint or summarize state laws on specific topics. These include books, compendia, websites, and law review articles, which often have footnotes surveying state code provisions. A valuable resource called *Subject Compilations of State Laws*, available through HeinOnline, describes these collections and lists of state statutes. The online version is cumulative and has links to law review articles in HeinOnline as well as to publicly available Internet sites. *Subject Compilations* does not itself summarize or cite the statutes, but it has annotated descriptions of sources that do.

d. Uniform Laws

Most multistate research requires finding a wide variety of legislative approaches to a particular topic. In a growing number of areas, however, states have adopted virtually identical acts. This can dramatically reduce the confusion caused by conflicting state statutes. The National Conference of Commissioners on Uniform State Laws (NCCUSL) has drafted more than three hundred laws designed to decrease unnecessary conflicts. Most of these are in force in at least one state, and some (such as the Uniform Commercial Code or Uniform Child Custody Jurisdiction Act) have been enacted in virtually every jurisdiction.

Uniform Laws Annotated, a multivolume set published by West and available on Westlaw, contains every uniform law approved by the NCCUSL, lists of adopting states, Commissioners' comments, and annotations to court decisions from adopting jurisdictions. These annotations allow researchers in one state to study the case law developed in other states with the same uniform law. A decision from another state is not binding authority, but its interpretation of identical or similar language may be persuasive. The printed set is supplemented annually by the pamphlet *Directory of Uniform Acts and Codes; Tables-Index*, which lists the acts alphabetically and includes a table of jurisdictions indicating the acts adopted in each state. Uniform acts, with comments but not case annotations, are also available from Lexis and Bloomberg Law.

The text of a uniform law can also be found, of course, in the statutory code of each adopting state, with annotations from that state's courts. The state code contains the law as actually adopted and in force, which may not be identical to the text as proposed by the Commissioners. The NCCUSL version is merely a proposal, but the state code version is the law.

The texts of most uniform acts, fact sheets indicating the status of state adoption, and information about current projects are available online from the NCCUSL website (www.uniformlaws.org). The Legal Information Institute has "Uniform Law Locators" (www.law.cornell.edu/uniform/), listing links to official sites where the text as adopted in particular states can be found.

Model acts are drafted for areas of law where individual states are expected to modify a proposed law to meet their needs, rather than adopt it as drafted. The American Law Institute has produced the Model Penal Code and other model acts; the American Bar Association is responsible for the Revised Model Business Corporation Act. Research resources for these acts include *Model Penal Code and Commentaries* (1980–85) and *Model Business Corporation Act Annotated* (4th ed. 2008–date), which is available on Bloomberg Law.

e. Interstate Compacts

An interstate compact is an agreement between two or more states, which under the Constitution requires approval by Congress. Compacts generally appear in the *U.S. Statutes at Large* and in the session laws and codes for the states that are parties. The National Center for Interstate Compacts (www. csg.org/ncic/) has a variety of useful resources on the subject, including background information and a searchable database of more than 1,500 compacts in state codes.

§ 4–6.   The U.S. Constitution

The United States Constitution is the basic law of the country, defining political relationships, enumerating the rights and liberties of citizens, and creating the framework of national government. Unlike statutes, which are often written in extreme detail and specificity, the Constitution contains concise statements of broad principles. It entered into force in March 1789, and in more than two centuries it has been amended only twenty-seven times. Among the most important of these amendments are the Bill of Rights, guaranteeing personal liberties, and the Fourteenth Amendment, applying these protections to the states.

Although its text has changed little, courts have applied the Constitution to numerous situations that its drafters could not have foreseen. In interpreting constitutional provisions, it is particularly important to examine relevant decisions of the Supreme Court and the lower federal courts. Judicial interpretations of constitutional principles can be just as significant as the express language of the Constitution.

The text of the Constitution appears in numerous publications ranging from simple pamphlets to standard reference works such as *Black's Law Dictionary*, and it is available at dozens of Internet sites. It is also printed at the beginning of the *United States Code*, the official publication of federal statutes. As with statutes, however, the two annotated publications, *United States Code Annotated* (*USCA*) and *United States Code Service* (*USCS*), are far more useful in legal research. These publications, available in print and on Westlaw or Lexis, have much more than just the text of the Constitution. Each clause is accompanied by notes of decisions, arranged by subject and thoroughly indexed. Some major provisions have thousands of notes in several hundred subject divisions. The Constitution is so heavily annotated that it occupies twenty-eight volumes in *USCA* and ten volumes in *USCS*. These exhaustive annotations make *USCA* and *USCS* essential resources in determining how the Constitution's broad principles have been applied to specific circumstances.

Of the many commentaries on the Constitution, one of the broadest and most readily available is *The Constitution of the United States of America: Analysis and Interpretation*. Prepared by the Congressional Research Service of the Library of Congress, this work is published as a Senate Document every ten years and is updated annually online (www.gpo.gov/constitutionannotated). It is a useful starting point for constitutional research, with a thorough analysis of Supreme Court decisions applying each provision and footnotes citing scholarly monographs and law review articles.

Other helpful background sources include *Encyclopedia of the American Constitution* (Leonard W. Levy & Kenneth L. Karst eds., 2d ed. 2000) and *Encyclopedia of the Supreme Court of the United States* (David S. Tanenhaus ed., 2008), both of which include articles on constitutional doctrines as well as on specific court decisions, people, and historical periods. *The Oxford Companion to the Supreme Court of the United States* (Kermit Hall ed., 2d ed. 2005) is a shorter work with similar treatment of constitutional issues. *The Oxford Handbook of the U.S. Constitution* (Mark Tushnet et al. eds., 2015) has in-depth treatment of about four dozen major topics.

For further historical research, you can turn to the documents prepared by those who drafted, adopted, and ratified the Constitution. There was no official record of the debates in the constitutional convention, but Max Farrand's *The Records of the Federal Convention of 1787* (1911 & 1987 supp.) is considered the most authoritative source for the notes of James Madison and other participants. The traditional source for the state ratification debates is Jonathan Elliot, *The Debates in the Several State Conventions on the Adoption of the Federal Constitution* (2d ed., 1836–45). The Library of Congress website provides access to both Farrand's *Records* and Elliot's *Debates* (memory.loc.gov/ammem/amlaw/). A more comprehensive modern treatment, *The Documentary History of the Ratification of the Constitution* (Merrill Jensen et al. eds., 1976–date) (rotunda.upress.virginia.edu/founders/), contains debates, commentaries and other documents.

John R. Vile, *The Constitutional Convention of 1787: A Comprehensive Encyclopedia of America's Founding* (2005), is a convenient start point for research. *The Founders' Constitution* (Philip B. Kurland & Ralph Lerner eds., 1987) (press-pubs.uchicago.edu/founders/) and *The Complete Bill of Rights: The Drafts, Debates, Sources, and Origins* (Neil H. Cogan ed., 2d ed. 2015) are useful collections of excerpts from source documents arranged by the constitutional provision to which they apply.

§ 4–7.   State Constitutions

Each state is governed by its own constitution, which establishes the structure of government and guarantees fundamental rights. While state constitutions are roughly comparable to their federal counterpart, they tend to be much more detailed and generally are amended far more frequently. Some states have adopted new constitutions several times.

State constitutions can be important sources in cases involving individual rights. While a state cannot deprive citizens of federal constitutional rights, its constitution can guarantee rights beyond those provided under the U.S. Constitution. Just as the U.S. Supreme Court is the arbiter of the scope of protections offered by the federal constitution, the state court of last resort determines the scope of its constitution.

The best source for a state constitution is usually the annotated state code, which provides both the latest text and notes of court decisions interpreting and construing constitutional provisions. Unannotated constitutions are available online from state government sites.

Oxford Constitutions of the World (oxcon.ouplaw.com) is a comprehensive source for the texts of state constitutions, which are also available in print in *Constitutions of the United States, National and State* (2d ed. 1974–date). The best collection of historical state constitutions, *Constitutional Documents of the United States of America 1776–1860* (Horst Dippel ed., 2006–11) (www.modern-constitutions.de), only covers the period before the Civil War but it includes meticulously verified versions of all early texts. Later constitutions can be found in the microfiche *Constitutions of the World 1850 to the Present, Part 2: North and South America* (Horst Dippel ed., 2005).

Robert L. Maddex, *State Constitutions of the United States* (2d ed. 2006) and *The Constitutionalism of American States* (George E. Connor & Christopher W. Hammons eds., 2008) are useful sources for surveying constitutional provisions between states, with chapters on the constitutional history and theory of each state. The first chapter of the Council of State Governments' annual *Book of the States* (knowledgecenter.csg.org) also has tables on topics such as the length of each constitution, dates of adoption, and amendment procedures.

For research into a particular state's constitution, one of the best starting is the *Oxford Commentaries on the State Constitutions of the United States* (originally published as *Reference Guides to the State Constitutions*), a series of monographs covering almost every state. Each volume includes a summary of the state's constitutional history, a detailed section-by-section analysis of the constitution with background information and discussion of judicial interpretations, and a brief bibliographical essay providing references for further research.

Journals and proceedings of state constitutional conventions can provide insight into framers' intent. The lack of indexing in many older volumes can make research difficult, but digitized versions may be searchable by keyword. The most comprehensive source for such documents is the ProQuest collection *State Constitutional Conventions on Microfiche (1776–1988)*, containing material from all fifty states. You can also find information on resources for territorial and early state constitutions in *Prestatehood Legal Materials: A Fifty-State Research Guide* (Michael Chiorazzi & Marguerite Most eds., 2005).

CHAPTER 5

LEGISLATIVE INFORMATION

Images of some resources discussed in this chapter are at **libguides.law.virginia.edu/nutshell12/ch5**

---

§ 5–1. Introduction

Statutory language is often ambiguous, and lawyers and scholars frequently try to discern the intended purpose of an act or the meaning of particular terminology through the legislative documents created during its enactment. Researchers also need to investigate the progress of proposed laws as legislatures consider them. These processes—

determining the meaning of an enacted law and ascertaining the status of a pending bill—comprise legislative history research.

The use of legislative history in statutory construction is controversial, with strong disagreement within the Supreme Court and among scholars. Judges have traditionally used congressional materials to interpret ambiguous statutory language, but textualist critics insist that meaning must be determined from the statutory language alone. Despite this criticism, most judges rely on legislative history sources to correct drafting errors, to provide information on specialized meanings of terms, and to identify the purpose of a statutory phrase.

There can be striking differences between federal and state legislative history research. Congressional action is thoroughly documented with numerous sources, while the lack of available information can make state legislative history research quite frustrating. Information on pending and recent legislation is readily available from federal and state government websites. Research into the background of older acts of Congress, however, requires access to either commercial services or printed sources, and resources on older state laws, if they exist at all, may be found only on tape recordings or in archives at the state capitol.

§ 5–2.   Federal Legislative History Sources

The documents of legislative history must be understood in the context of the legislative process that produces them. The federal process is often long and complicated, beginning formally with the introduction of a bill and ending with passage by both houses of Congress and approval by the President (or repassage over a presidential veto).

Guides to federal lawmaking procedures include Walter J. Oleszek et al., *Congressional Procedures and the Policy Process* (10th ed. 2016), and Charles Tiefer, *Congressional Practice and Procedure: A Reference, Research, and Legislative Guide* (1989). Congressional Quarterly's *Guide to Congress* (7th ed. 2012) has a wide range of political, historical, and statistical information; Part III, Congressional Procedures, is particularly useful in understanding committee and floor action.

Each stage in the enactment of a federal law may result in a significant legislative history document. The most important potential steps in the legislative process and their related documents are:

Action	**Document**
Preliminary inquiry	Transcripts of hearings on the general subject of the proposed legislation
Executive recommendation	Presidential message proposing an administration bill
Introduction of bill and referral to committee	Slip bill as introduced
Hearings on bill	Transcript of testimony and exhibits

Action	Document
Action	**Document**
Approval by committee	Committee report, including committee's version of bill
Legislative debates	*Congressional Record*, sometimes including texts of bill in amended forms
Passage by first house	Engrossed bill (final House or Senate version of the proposed legislation)
Consideration by other house	Generally same procedure and documents as above
Referral to conference committee (if texts passed by houses differ)	Conference committee version of bill; conference committee report
Passage of identical bill by both houses	Enrolled bill sent to President
Approval by President	Presidential signing statement; slip law, subsequently published in *Statutes at Large* and classified by subject in the *U.S. Code*

Of the many types of documents issued by Congress, a few are particularly important for legislative history research. *Bills* are the major source for the texts of pending or unenacted legislation. *Committee reports* analyze and describe bills and are usually considered the most authoritative sources of congressional intent. *Floor debates* may contain a sponsor's interpretation of a bill or the only explanation of last-minute amendments. *Hearings* can provide useful background on the purpose of an act.

This section introduces these various documents, with a brief explanation of how they are published and their availability in electronic sources including Congress.gov (www.congress.gov), the Library of Congress website for legislative information, and the Government Printing Office's Federal Digital System (FDsys) (www.gpo.gov/fdsys/), as well as commercial online sites. Section 5–3 looks in greater depth at using these and other sources for legislative history research.

a. Bills

The texts of bills are needed by researchers interested in pending or failed legislation, and may also help in interpreting enacted laws. Comparing the different versions of a bill may lead to useful conclusions about the scope or meaning of the provisions that were ultimately enacted. If a provision you are studying was added after a bill was introduced, pinpointing the date of its insertion can help you determine the most pertinent legislative history sources.

Bills are numbered in separate series for each chamber, and retain their identifying numbers through both sessions of a Congress. A pending bill lapses at the end of the two-year term, and a new bill must be introduced if it is to be considered the following term.

Some public laws arise from *joint resolutions* rather than bills. These usually, but not always, deal with matters of a limited or temporary nature. Joint resolutions and bills differ in form but have the same legal effect. Two other forms of resolution do not have the force of law: *concurrent resolutions* expressing the opinion of both chambers of Congress, and *simple resolutions* concerning the procedures or expressions of just one chamber.

Often bills with similar or identical language, known as *companion bills*, are introduced in both House and Senate. If each chamber passes its own bill, however, there is no single *enrolled bill* that has passed both chambers and can be presented to the President. Congress frequently employs a procedure known as an *amendment in the nature of a substitute*, which deletes everything after the enacting clause ("Be it enacted by the Senate and House of Representatives of the United States of America in Congress assembled") and inserts new text in its place. Sometimes this is done simply because it is more convenient to replace an entire bill than to make specific changes, but it also makes it easier for the House and Senate to pass the same bill so that it can go to the President and become law. The significance of this for researchers is that the number of the bill that becomes law may be different from the number of the proposed bill that was the subject of congressional hearings, committee reports, or perhaps even floor debates. The key language in an enacted law may have come from a different bill with a different set of legislative history documents.

Bills are available online from several sources. The most extensive source is ProQuest Digital U.S. Bills and Resolutions, 1789–Present, a component of ProQuest Congressional. Congress.gov and FDsys both have the text of recent bills, beginning with the 103rd Congress (1993–94). Lexis coverage begins in 1989, Bloomberg Law in 1993, and Westlaw in 1995.

b. Committee Reports

Reports are generally considered the most important sources of legislative history. They are issued by House and Senate committees on bills they approve and send to the floor for consideration, and usually include the text of the bill, describe its contents and purposes, and give reasons for the committee's recommendations, sometimes with minority views. One of the most informative portions of a committee report is the section-by-section analysis of the bill, explaining the purpose and meaning of each provision.

Conference committee reports, issued by the group of representatives and senators convened to reconcile differences between bills passed by the two chambers, are considered a very persuasive source for interpretation. Because they generally only consider points of difference between the two bills, however, conference committee reports do not discuss bill provisions as exhaustively as House or Senate committee reports.

Committee reports are identified by chamber, Congress, and report number, with conference committee reports included in the series of House reports. The committee reports for a session are collected, along with House and Senate Documents, in an official compilation called the *Serial Set*. (Bound *Serial Set* volumes after 1996 are not widely distributed, but some libraries bind their own sets of individual reports.) Congress.gov, FDsys, and Bloomberg Law coverage begins in 1995, and Westlaw and Lexis have all committee reports beginning in 1990 as well as selected earlier reports. The ProQuest U.S. Serial Set Digital Collection, covering 1789–date, and Readex's U.S. Congressional Serial Set (1817–1994) have retrospective, full-text digital coverage, and selected reports are also reprinted in *United States Code Congressional and Administrative News* (*USCCAN*).

Reports are the final product of committee deliberation, and are more widely available than the transcripts of *markup sessions*, the meetings in which committees reach consensus. These can be significant sources of legislative intent if they are published or available online on committee websites. Newspapers and wire services reporting on Capitol Hill provide coverage of markup sessions, but without official transcripts the value of these articles as legislative history is limited.

c. Debates

As sources of legislative intent, debates in the House and Senate are generally not as influential as committee reports. While reports represent the considered opinion of those legislators who have studied a bill most closely, floor statements are often political hyperbole and may represent the views of the proposed legislation's opponents. The most influential statements are those from a bill's sponsor or its floor managers (the committee members responsible for steering the bill through consideration).

In a few instances, floor debates are the best available legislative history source. Bills can be amended on the floor, sometimes with language that was not considered in committee and thus was not discussed in a committee report. If so, the record of floor debate may be the only available explanation of the intended purpose of an amendment.

The source for debates is the *Congressional Record*, published each day that either chamber is in session. Each daily issue has separately paginated "H" and "S" sections for House and Senate proceedings. The *Record* provides a more or less verbatim transcript of the legislative debates and proceedings, but legislators have the opportunity to revise their remarks and to insert material that was not actually spoken. Material that was not spoken is generally indicated in the House proceedings by a different typeface. Some inserted text in the Senate proceedings is indicated by the use of bullet symbols, but extended colloquies can be added without any indication that they were never heard on the floor of the Senate.

The *Congressional Record* includes the text of conference committee reports, but it rarely reprints other committee reports. Bills are sometimes printed in the *Record*, particularly if they have been amended on the floor or in conference committee. The

Congressional Record's primary role, however, is as a report of debates and actions taken.

Each *Congressional Record* issue contains a Daily Digest summarizing the day's activities. The digest lists the bills introduced, reports filed, measures debated or passed, and committee meetings held. A cumulative index and a History of Bills and Resolutions table, with status information and page references for each bill, are available on the FDsys website.

The daily edition of the *Congressional Record* is available through several online sources. Coverage begins in 1989 on Congress.gov, and in 1994 from FDsys. Congress.gov's version has links from the index and Daily Digest to *Record* pages and to bill texts, while FDsys has the *Record* in PDF format replicating the printed version. Westlaw and Lexis coverage extends back to 1985, and Bloomberg Law has the daily edition back to 1989.

A bound permanent edition of the *Congressional Record* is published several years after the end of each session. Once the permanent edition is published, it becomes the standard source to be cited for congressional debates. The daily and permanent editions have the same volume numbers, but the permanent edition renumbers the separate House and Senate pages into one sequence.

Neither Westlaw nor Lexis has the permanent edition of the *Congressional Record*, but it is available online from other sources. Bloomberg Law has the permanent edition from 1933 to 1988, and

HeinOnline and the ProQuest Congressional Record Permanent Digital Collection both have retrospective coverage back to the first volume in 1873. HeinOnline and ProQuest have date-matching tools with which you can convert a daily edition citation to a permanent edition citation, easing what has in the past been an onerous process, but these do not yet cover the entire range of the *Record*. To find the permanent edition citation without these tools, you would need to search for specific text or look for references to the topic or speaker in the index or the Daily Digest.

The predecessors of the *Congressional Record* are the *Annals of Congress* (1789–1824); the *Register of Debates* (1824–37); and the *Congressional Globe* (1833–73). All of these earlier publications, as well as the *Congressional Record* for 1873–77, are available online through the Library of Congress's "A Century of Lawmaking for a New Nation" site (memory.loc. gov/ammem/amlaw/), as well as from HeinOnline and ProQuest.

House and *Senate Journals* are also published (and are, in fact, the only congressional publications required by the Constitution). These do not, however, include the text of debates, but merely record the proceedings and report the resulting action and votes taken. The *House Journal* also includes the texts of bills and amendments given floor consideration, and both journals have History of Bills and Resolutions tables and indexes. *House Journal* volumes back to 1992 are available through FDsys.

d. Hearings

House and Senate committees hold hearings on proposed legislation and on other subjects under congressional investigation such as nominations or impeachments. Government officials, scholars, and interest group representatives deliver prepared statements and answer questions from committee members. Hearings are not required for every bill, and legislation is frequently enacted without hearings in one or both chambers.

Hearings have useful background information, but they are not generally considered persuasive sources of legislative history on the meaning of an enacted bill. Their importance as evidence of legislative intent is limited because they focus more on the views of interested parties rather than those of the lawmakers themselves.

The transcripts of most hearings are published, accompanied by submitted material such as letters and article reprints. Searchable PDFs of these hearings, with selected coverage beginning in 1995, are available from FDsys, as well as through Bloomberg Law. The major retrospective online source is the ProQuest Congressional Hearings Digital Collection, with more than 120,000 hearings back to 1824. The full text of the hearings is searchable, and witnesses can be found by name or affiliation. HeinOnline's U.S. Congressional Documents Library has more than 24,000 hearings, most from the 1950s to date.

Unlike committee reports, hearings are not issued in one numbered series for each chamber. Instead they are generally identified by the title on the cover, the name of the subcommittee and committee, the term of Congress, and the year.

Most committee websites, linked from the Senate (www.senate.gov) and House (www.house.gov) sites, have prepared statements of legislators and witnesses from current hearings. Westlaw and Lexis usually have witnesses' statements and commercially prepared transcripts well before the official versions are published.

e. Other Congressional Publications

Congress also produces other publications that are less frequently consulted in legislative history research. These can be important sources of information, however, on statutes, legislative policies, and the workings of the federal government.

Committee Prints. These contain a variety of material prepared for committee use, ranging from staff studies to compilations of legislative history documents. Some prints contain statements by committee members on pending bills. Others can be useful analyses of laws under a committee's jurisdiction, such as the House's biennial *Green Book* on programs within the jurisdiction of the Committee on Ways and Means. Committee prints are not as widely available online as reports or hearings. Selective coverage back to the mid-1990s is available through FDsys, Bloomberg Law, and Lexis. The most comprehensive source is the ProQuest Congressional

Research Digital Collection, which includes thousands of committee prints dating back to 1830.

House and Senate Documents. These include the *Budget of the United States Government*, special studies or exhibits prepared for Congress, presidential messages, and communications from executive agencies. They are issued in a numbered series for each chamber as part of the official *Serial Set*, and are available starting in 1995 through FDsys, Bloomberg Law, and Lexis. Older documents are available through the ProQuest U.S. Serial Set Digital Collection and Readex's U.S. Congressional Serial Set (1817–1994).

Treaty Documents and Senate Executive Reports. The Senate issues two series of publications in the process of treaty ratification. *Treaty documents* have the texts of treaties before the Senate for its advice and consent, and *Senate executive reports* contain the Foreign Relations Committee's recommendations on pending treaties. These publications are discussed more fully in Chapter 9.

Legislative Agencies. Congress also supervises three major investigative and research agencies that produce a range of important analyses and reports. The Congressional Budget Office (CBO) (www.cbo. gov) produces cost estimates for bills reported out of committee as well as a variety of reports, analytical studies, and background papers. The Government Accountability Office (GAO) (www.gao.gov) (formerly the General Accounting Office) studies the programs and expenditures of the federal government, and frequently recommends specific congressional actions. The CBO and GAO websites have reports and other documents, and GAO reports back to 1994 are also available through FDsys, Westlaw, Bloomberg Law, and Lexis.

The most wide-ranging research arm of Congress is the Congressional Research Service (CRS). Each year it produces several thousand reports, including legal and policy analyses, economic studies, bibliographies, statistical reviews, and issue briefs with background information on major legislative issues. The CRS has no publicly accessible website and does not publish its reports, but they are regularly made available by others. Reports back to 1916 are available through the subscription-based ProQuest Congressional Research Digital Collection, and Bloomberg Law has coverage of new reports beginning in 2011. Free access is provided by the University of North Texas Digital Library (digital. library.unt.edu/explore/collections/crsr/) and other sites.

§ 5–3.   Congressional Research Resources

While researchers are interested in Congress for numerous reasons, this discussion focuses on tools useful for two important legal research tasks: investigating the meaning of an enacted law, and tracking the status of pending legislation. You can use a number of approaches for these purposes. For recently enacted laws and pending legislation, several electronic resources are available. For older bills, the choices dwindle to a few tools with retrospective coverage.

Sometimes you may undertake legislative history research to get a general understanding of a law, but more often you will be looking for clues to interpret specific language in a code section. You will be looking for documentation as close as possible to the time when decisions were made to use the language you seek to interpret, such as the point at which it was added by amendment or the point at which it was voted on. You will be looking for statements by the supporters of the language rather than its opponents, if there was a debate.

Be warned that this can be a frustrating endeavor. Even after finding all the relevant materials on a statute, you may learn that the legislature never explained or discussed the particular language you are researching. Legislative history is just one of several tools used in statutory interpretation.

The increasing use of omnibus legislation and unorthodox procedures has also made legislative history research more difficult. Especially towards the end of a legislative session, numerous bills may be combined into mammoth enactments of several hundred pages. Materials addressing a provision within a huge omnibus bill can be much more difficult to locate than those on a bill with one discrete subject. In other instances bills bypass the committee process and go directly to the floor for consideration, meaning that there may be no relevant committee reports or hearings.

The bill number is usually the key to finding congressional documents or tracing legislative action. It appears in brackets at the beginning of each enacted law, both in its slip form and in the *Statutes at Large*. Bill numbers have been included in *Statutes at Large* volumes since 1903; earlier numbers can be found in Eugene Nabors, *Legislative Reference Checklist* (1982, available on HeinOnline). Bill numbers are not listed in the *United States Code* or in either of its annotated editions.

Which legislative history research resources to use in any particular circumstance depends on the date of the law and the scope of information you need. The most up-to-date information on current legislation is found in Congress.gov or one of the other online bill-tracking services. The most comprehensive coverage of documents relating to enacted laws is usually found in ProQuest resources. The quickest way to find and evaluate committee reports may be to read through those reprinted in *USCCAN*. For legislative history information on older laws, the *Congressional Record*'s History of Bills and Resolutions, which dates back to the nineteenth century, may be the only available resource. A compiled legislative history, if available, may have done most of your work for you.

One of the most useful resources in legislative history research is the Law Librarians' Society of Washington, D.C.'s Legislative Source Book (www. llsdc.org/sourcebook/). This site includes features such as links to congressional committee publications, questions and answers on legislative research, and a practitioner's guide to compiling a federal legislative history.

a. Compiled Legislative Histories

Identifying and gathering the documents that make up a legislative history can be a time-consuming process, and a resource that has already compiled these documents can make the research process much easier. Such resources, online and in print, are available for many federal acts.

The most exhaustive source of compiled legislative histories is ProQuest Legislative Insight (li.proquest. com/legislativeinsight), a subscription resource that covers more than 27,000 laws dating back to 1789. Its coverage is not yet complete, but for laws within its scope it has PDFs of all relevant bills, reports, hearings, debate, and other documents. Rather than limiting coverage to a single term of Congress, it collects relevant bills, reports, and hearings from prior terms. The documents for a complex and lengthy act can span several years and include hundreds of items. The full text of all documents for an enactment can be searched simultaneously for specific phrases or combinations of words. Documents that match the search request are indicated, but they must be downloaded and searched individually to see the context in which the terms appear.

HeinOnline's U.S. Federal Legislative History Library has searchable PDFs of documents for several hundred acts, including major legislation in areas such as environmental law, immigration, intellectual property, labor law, and taxation. This collection is based on William S. Hein & Company's publications of compiled legislative histories, which has volumes covering individual acts as well as more extensive sets such as *Congress and the Courts: A Legislative History 1787–2010* and *Internal Revenue Acts of the United States, 1909–1950.* Printed legislative history compilations have also been issued by government agencies charged with the enforcement of particular acts and by interested groups such as trade associations.

Westlaw and Lexis have compiled legislative histories, including bills and committee reports, for major acts in areas such as bankruptcy, tax, and environmental law. Westlaw also has a "U.S. GAO Federal Legislative Histories" collection, with several thousand legislative history summaries for acts from 1915 to 1995. These compilations list reports, *Congressional Record* excerpts, and hearings; most documents are available in PDF and are searchable.

You can determine what legislative histories are available on Westlaw, Lexis, and HeinOnline through the Legislative Source Book's "Commercial Legislative Histories of U.S. Laws on the Internet" page (www.llsdc.org/leg-hist-commercial), which includes links to the sources it lists. Nancy P. Johnson's *Sources of Compiled Legislative Histories* (3d ed. 2014), available as part of HeinOnline's U.S. Federal Legislative History Library, has a checklist of print and online sources for acts as far back as 1789. It covers not only collections that reprint the documents but also law review articles and other sources that list and discuss the relevant materials.

b. Congress.gov and Other Government Websites

For current legislation or laws enacted since 1973, one of the easiest places to begin research is Congress.gov, the official site for legislative information. Congress.gov has the text of bills as well as summaries of their status or legislative history. You can search by either keyword or bill number, and then filter search results by Congress, status, subject, or any of several other criteria. A bill's summary is accompanied by tabs linking to text versions, legislative actions, amendments, and related bills. While legislative history summaries are available for laws enacted since 1973, summaries for older laws lack some of the features included for more recent legislation. Links to the text of legislation are available beginning in 1989, and *Congressional Record* page references and links begin in 1993.

Congress.gov also includes links to the Government Printing Office's FDsys website (www.gpo.gov/fdsys/), which provides these documents as PDF files. FDsys is the more comprehensive source for documents, but it has no links between its congressional documents and does not provide bill summaries or status information.

The House (www.house.gov) and Senate (www.senate.gov) websites have general information on congressional activity, as well as links to pages for individual members and committees. Most committee homepages have summaries of major pending legislation, background information, hearing statements, and schedules of upcoming meetings.

c. ProQuest Congressional

In 1970 Congressional Information Service, a private company, began indexing congressional publications and providing copies of these publications in microform. These indexes and documents are now available online through ProQuest Congressional (congressional.proquest.com).

Proquest Congressional indexes virtually all congressional publications since 1789, with full-text copies available of most publications it lists. Unlike Legislative Insight, it covers reports and hearings on bills that were never enacted as well as documents unrelated to legislation.

ProQuest Congressional has abstracts of all available reports, hearings, prints, and documents. Hearing abstracts, for example, indicate the names and affiliations of witnesses and the focus of their testimony, so that you can track the appearances of a particular agency or interest group.

In addition to abstracting individual congressional publications, ProQuest Congressional also has legislative history summaries for each enacted law since 1970, listing relevant bills, hearings, reports, debates, presidential documents and any other legislative actions. Like the ProQuest Legislative Insight legislative histories, these summaries do not limit coverage to a single term of Congress but include references to earlier hearings and other documents on related bills from prior Congressional sessions. The difference between the two resources is that Legislative Insight collects the material so that it can all be searched together while Congressional merely lists (and provides links to) documents that must then be retrieved individually.

Acts before 1970 are not covered in ProQuest Congressional by legislative history summaries, but the thorough retrospective indexing means that reports and hearings on a particular bill are linked to that bill. You can search for documents associated with a bill by using the Search by Number feature. This isn't always comprehensive, so it should be supplemented by keyword searching or other approaches.

Other features of ProQuest Congressional include bill-tracking summaries; full-text access to bills, reports, the *Congressional Record*, and other congressional documents beginning in the 1980s; transcripts of hearing testimony; and information on committees and legislators.

d. USCCAN *and Westlaw*

United States Code Congressional and Administrative News (*USCCAN*) is a print publication that reprints one or more committee reports for most acts, making it a convenient source for basic legislative research. *USCCAN* generally prints either a House or Senate report and the conference committee report, if one was issued. *USCCAN* is often available in smaller libraries with limited collections of congressional materials, and *The Bluebook* advises that report citations include *USCCAN* references "when possible."

USCCAN has been printing committee reports since 1941. Westlaw has the reports reprinted in *USCCAN* beginning in 1948, and all congressional committee reports since 1990, including reports on bills that did not become law.

References to *USCCAN* legislative histories are included in the notes in the *United States Code Annotated*. Westlaw's version of *USCA* has links under "Editor's and Revisor's Notes" on the History tab to the *USCCAN* summary and reports, making it easy to get from a code section to the committee reports. Note, however, that a reference after a specific section means only that legislative history on the act as a whole is available, not that pertinent material on that specific section will be found.

USCCAN has only selective coverage of committee reports, and further research is often required. There are no references to hearings, prints, documents, or materials from previous Congresses, so anyone preparing a complete legislative history will need to use other resources. But it is a handy starting point, and the material in *USCCAN* may be sufficient if all you need is general background or a quick section-by-section analysis.

As noted earlier, Westlaw also has resources such as bill texts, committee reports, and the *Congressional Record* for laws enacted since the 1990s. These are linked to *USCA* code sections under the "Legislative History Materials" section of the History tab. As with the *USCCAN* references, however, these links do not necessarily refer to the specific section.

e. CQ and Other Tracking Services

Newspapers and services that cover Congress and politics are often good sources on congressional action, providing information that may not be available from official documentation. Even if a bill appears to be stalled in committee, news stories and press releases can provide leads to what is happening behind the scenes.

CQ Roll Call is a news service and publisher of several sources of information on congressional activity including *CQ Weekly* (formerly *Congressional Quarterly Weekly Report*), which provides background information on pending legislation and news of current developments. *CQ Weekly* does not include the texts of documents or comprehensive bill-tracking, but it has useful analysis and background discussion of laws and legislative issues.

CQ Weekly contains tables of House and Senate votes and a status table for major legislation. An annual *CQ Almanac Plus* cumulates much of the information in the *Weekly* into a useful summary of the congressional session, and the series *Congress and the Nation* has broader multiyear coverage. More frequent publications for current congressional news include *CQ Today* and CQ Midday Update, which is available free by e-mail.

For academic and public libraries, CQ Press Electronic Library (library.cqpress.com) provides a subscription-based online version of *CQ Weekly* and related reference works. *CQ Weekly* is also available on Westlaw, with coverage beginning in 2005.

Numerous other newspapers and magazines also focus on developments in Washington. In addition to general news sources, specialized publications include *CongressDaily*, *National Journal*, and *Roll Call*. Westlaw has *CongressDaily* and *Roll Call*, and all three publications are available through Lexis. Some sources, such as *The Hill* (www.thehill.com), are available on the Internet without charge.

Free resources such as Govtrack.us (www.govtrack.us) and OpenCongress (www.opencongress.org) can also track current legislation. Bills can be searched by keyword, and the results show a bill's progress and link to its text. Registered users can sign up to receive updates about pending bills.

Online subscription services including CQ Roll Call (cqrollcall.com) also provide information on Congress, including bill tracking and committee markup reports. Designed for specialists in current congressional information, these services offer a range of sophisticated tracking and notification services unavailable from free government sites and more general online resources.

f. Status Tables

For the purpose of tracking current legislation and researching recently enacted laws, online resources have advantages of convenience and speed that are unmatched in print. For earlier bills and laws, however, printed resources may still be the best available sources of information.

Congressional Index **(CCH) (1937–date).** This looseleaf service's coverage of proposed legislation indexes bills by subject and author and has a status table of actions taken on each bill. *Congressional Index*, published since the 75th Congress in 1937–38, is one of the most comprehensive sources of information on bills predating the coverage of online bill-tracking services. Its status tables include references to hearings, a feature lacking in many other resources.

Congressional Index does not contain the texts of bills or reports, but it has a wide range of other information on Congress, including lists of members and committee assignments; an index of enactments and vetoes; lists of pending treaties, reorganization plans, and nominations; a table of voting records; and a weekly newsletter.

Congressional Record **and Earlier Status Tables (1789–date).** As noted earlier, the *Congressional Record* includes status tables that can be useful for both current and retrospective research. The final cumulative History of Bills and Resolutions, published in the index volume of the bound *Congressional Record* set, is a valuable resource because it uses the pagination of the bound volumes instead of the separate "S" and "H" pages in the daily edition. This makes it an easy way to locate a bound volume reference if needed for a citation. Although the History of Bills and Resolutions is less comprehensive than commercial sources, it remains one of the best sources available for older laws. These tables have been published annually since the 1867 volume of the *Congressional Globe*, long before the earliest coverage of most commercial publications.

The History of Bills table is available on FDsys back to 1983, with *Congressional Record* dates and citations beginning in 1993. The FDsys version, unfortunately, does not include links from its references to the documents listed.

For even earlier acts, the *House* and *Senate Journals* all the way back to the First Congress (1789–91) include tables or lists of bills indicating when they were reported, passed, or received other floor action. Most of these are found in the subject index under "Bills." The early journals are available online through the Library of Congress's "A Century of Lawmaking for a New Nation" site (memory.loc.gov/ammem/amlaw/).

g. Directories

In some instances, one of the fastest ways to find out about the status of pending legislation is to call congressional staff members responsible for drafting or monitoring the bill. They may be able to provide information or insights that would never appear in published status tables or reports. The best source for detailed information on staff members is a commercial directory, *Congressional Yellow Book*. It has addresses, telephone numbers, and (for some staff members) brief biographical information. An online version (www.leadershipdirectories.com) is updated daily.

The *Official Congressional Directory* is not as detailed as the *Yellow Book*, but it has information about individuals, offices, and the organizational structure of Congress. The online version of this directory, available through FDsys, is modified during the term to reflect changes.

Two useful sources for background information on members of Congress, both published biennially, are National Journal's *Almanac of American Politics* and *CQ's Politics in America*. These have in-depth biographical portraits with information on voting records and ratings from interest groups, as well as a brief narrative and statistical overview of each congressional district.

A retrospective Biographical Directory of the United States Congress, 1774–Present (including coverage of the Continental Congress) is available online (bioguide.congress.gov), and provides basic information on the more than 13,000 people who have served in Congress. A printed version of the same resource, under the title *Biographical Directory of the American Congress, 1774–1996* (1997), covers the 1st through 104th Congresses. Although it is less current than the online version, it has useful Congress-by-Congress directories of congressional leaders and state delegations. These include footnotes indicating deaths, resignations, and other changes.

§ 5–4. State Legislative Information

Legislative history on the state level is a research area of sharp contrasts. Information on current legislation is widely available online, but documents that might aid in the interpretation of enacted laws can be difficult to find or unavailable. Many states have never published resources such as committee reports or legislative debates.

First the good news: Most state legislatures provide convenient online access to current status information and to the text of pending bills. The better websites have several means of searching for bills, and some offer e-mail notification services when particular bills are acted upon. Some states offer other features such as bill summaries, committee minutes, and staff analyses.

Legislative websites can be found by using a search engine to find "[state] legislature" or from state homepages. The National Conference of State Legislatures (www.ncsl.org) has a page with links to legislative websites, from which you can either go directly to a specific site or create a customized multistate list of links for specific content such as bill information or legislator biographies.

Many legislative websites include an introductory guide to the state's lawmaking process. State legislatures generally follow the federal paradigm, but there can be significant differences from state to state. An important first step in studying legislative action in a particular state is to learn about its procedures. Guides and resources such as charts showing how bills become law can save you considerable time and confusion.

Commercial services also have bill texts and status information for pending state legislation. Westlaw, for example, has Proposed Legislation and Bill Tracking databases for each state, as well as a multistate Bill Tracking resource that can monitor developments in legislatures throughout the country. Historical Proposed Legislation coverage extends in most states back to the early 1990s.

For most states, Westlaw also has legislative history documents such as reports, bill analyses, legislative journals, and committee reports. Contents vary from state to state depending on the materials available. In Westlaw's statutory display, Legislative History Materials are listed under the History tab if a code section is derived from an act for which documents are available. As with federal statutes, however, a link does not necessarily mean that there is relevant information on the particular section. Coverage generally begins in the late 1990s or early 2000s.

Govtrack.us (www.govtrack.us) and Open States (openstates. org) are free websites that allow users to search and track pending legislation across all fifty states. The subscription site FiscalNote (www. fiscalnote.com) adds more sophisticated analysis tools.

Researchers needing to interpret statutes enacted before the late 1990s face a more difficult task. Bills from older sessions can be hard to locate. Almost every state has a legislative journal, but very few of these actually include transcripts of debates. Only a few states publish committee reports, and even fewer publish hearings.

In some states, reports and hearings are only available, if at all, at the state capitol. Some states have "bill jackets" with legislative information, and some have microform records or tape recordings of sessions. In many instances, contemporary newspaper accounts may be the best available source of information about proceedings or legislators' statements.

Several guides identify the resources available for each state. LLSDC's Legislative Source Book includes a "State Legislatures, State Laws, and State Regulations: Website Links and Telephone Numbers" page (www.llsdc.org/state-leg/), useful for quick links. The annual *State Legislative Sourcebook: A Resource Guide to Legislative Information in the Fifty States* has information on legislative processes and lists available published and online sources, including a "best initial contact" for each state, introductory guides, and bill tracking services. William H. Manz, *Guide to State Legislation, Legislative History, and Administrative Materials* (7th ed. 2008, available in HeinOnline) lists printed and online sources for bills and for legislative history materials, if available, such as hearings, reports, floor debates, and journals.

A guide to legislative research for a specific state can be invaluable. Most of the published state legal research guides listed in Appendix A discuss available legislative history resources for their states. State bar journals frequently publish articles on legislative history research. Law library websites in the jurisdiction you are researching, particularly the state legislative library if there is one, may have guides to doing legislative history research in their state. Indiana University's "State Legislative History Research Guides Inventory" (law.indiana.libguides. com/state-legislative-history-guides) has links to online guides from all fifty states.

A state research guide can also provide leads to official agencies responsible for recommending and drafting new legislation. These groups, including law revision commissions, judicial councils, and legislative councils, often publish annual or topical reports summarizing their work. For recommendations enacted into law, these reports may be valuable legislative history documentation.

Directory information on state legislatures, including organization, members, committees, and staffs, is contained in official state manuals (sometimes called *Bluebooks* or *Redbooks*), published annually or biennially by most states. Several multistate directories are also published, including *State Yellow Book* and the Council of State Governments' *CSG State Directory*.

In almost half of the states, statutes or constitutional amendments can bypass the legislature and be submitted directly to voters through the initiative process. Many states also permit popular referendums, ballot measures to reject measures enacted by the legislature. Information on the enactment and intent of these measures may not appear in the standard legislative history sources. The Initiative & Referendum Institute at the University of Southern California (www.iandrinstitute.org) has state-by-state information on the history and procedures of popular ballot measures, with links to state-specific sites. *Exploring Initiative and Referendum Law: Selected State Research Guides* (Beth Williams ed., 2007; also published as an issue of *Legal Reference Services Quarterly*) explains the initiative processes and research procedures in specific states.

Legislative materials are essential tools both in interpreting statutes and in monitoring current legal developments, but legislative history documents are hardly the only resources of value in understanding statutes. Court decisions may provide authoritative judicial interpretations, and many statutes are implemented by more detailed regulations and decisions from administrative agencies. These administrative materials, to be discussed in the next chapter, are key elements in understanding the application of the underlying statutes.

CHAPTER 6

ADMINISTRATIVE LAW

Images of some resources discussed in this chapter are at **libguides.law.virginia.edu/nutshell12/ch6**

---

§ 6–1.   Introduction

The executive is one of the three coordinate branches of government, but its lawmaking role was originally limited to orders and regulations needed to carry out the legislature's mandates. With the modern growth of government bureaucracy, however, the rules created by executive agencies are primary legal sources with pervasive impact. In many areas, administrative law can be more immediately relevant to day-to-day legal practice than either statutory or judge-made law.

Administrative law takes several forms, as lawmaking approaches and available resources vary by agency and subject area. Agencies can act both somewhat like legislatures and somewhat like courts. They may promulgate regulations governing activities within their jurisdiction, or they may decide matters involving particular litigants on a case-by-case basis. Part of becoming an expert in an area of law such as banking or immigration is learning about the idiosyncrasies of its administrative law materials.

Although executive agencies have existed in this country since its founding, the real growth of administrative law began in the late nineteenth century as the government sought to deal with the increasingly complex problems of industrialized society. In the 1930s, Congress created new regulatory agencies such as the Federal Communications Commission and the Securities and Exchange Commission to administer its New Deal programs. A third boom in administrative law occurred around 1970, as agencies such as the Environmental Protection Agency, the Consumer Product Safety Commission, and the Occupational Safety and Health Administration were created to address growing environmental and health concerns. The regulatory landscape continues to evolve, with the creation of the Department of

Homeland Security in 2002 and the Consumer Financial Protection Bureau in 2010.

Most of this chapter focuses on federal administrative law, but state agencies also play an important role. In addition, states delegate lawmaking responsibilities to counties and cities, which enact ordinances and have their own local agencies.

§ 6–2. Background Reference Sources

When researching administrative law, you need to determine what agency has jurisdiction and develop a preliminary understanding of its structure and functions. This may require a close reading of statutory and judicial sources to determine an agency's role. Most agencies are formed by legislation that defines their purpose and limits their parameters. You should understand an agency's legal mandates and information sources before delving into the documents it produces.

a. Agency Websites

An agency's website is often a convenient source of information on its history and current activities. Here, depending on the agency, you can usually find resources such as introductory overviews, organization charts, press releases, and directories. Much of this online information is not available in print.

Under the Electronic Freedom of Information Act Amendments of 1996, federal agency websites are required to include policy statements, interpretations, and staff instructions that affect the public.

The E-Government Act of 2002 further mandated that websites describe the agency's mission and organizational structure, and that they include a search function.

As a result of this legislation, an agency website is now the first place to look for information and documents. Website organization and transparency, however, vary considerably from agency to agency. Some agencies have clearly marked "Laws and Regulations" links at the top of their homepages, with easy access to relevant statutes, regulations, administrative decisions, and other documents. Others may have significant documents only in an "Electronic Reading Room" accessible by clicking on a "FOIA" link at the foot of the page. Some agency search engines are rather rudimentary, and you may achieve better results by using a general search engine such as Google and limiting results to a particular agency's site.

Most agency websites are easily found through web searches or by using an acronym and the domain *.gov* as a URL. USA.gov (www.usa.gov), the federal government's public portal, also has an A to Z Index with links to websites.

b. Guides and Directories

In order to decide which agency website to explore, you may need to do some background research to determine who has jurisdiction over a particular area. In other instances, you may want information that is unavailable from the agency site, such as contact information for specific personnel. For purposes such as these, federal government guides and directories can be valuable resources.

You can identify appropriate agencies in several ways. Cases or secondary sources may discuss administrative actions, or an annotated code may cite relevant regulations or decisions. CQ Press's annual *Washington Information Directory* is a guide to federal agencies, congressional committees, and nongovernmental organizations, listed by subject in nearly 100 areas such as education, employment and labor, energy, and environment and natural resources. Entries for agencies include brief descriptions, website addresses, and access information.

Once an agency is identified, general information about its structure, authority, and functions can be found in the *United States Government Manual*. This annual federal government directory, available both in print and online through the Government Printing Office's Federal Digital System (FDsys) (www.gpo.gov/fdsys/), cites the statutes under which an agency operates and explains its functions and major operating units. It has sources of information (including publications, telephone numbers, and websites) and organizational charts for most major agencies.

CQ Press's biennial *Federal Regulatory Directory* has a more extensive analysis of twelve major regulatory agencies, with shorter treatment of more than a hundred other agencies and offices. The coverage of each agency has a narrative introduction with historical background and a description of its programs, followed by listings of key personnel, information sources, and the major acts the agency administers.

To learn about the status of a particular regulation or enforcement activity, you may need to contact an agency directly by phone or e-mail. You should direct your inquiries as specifically as possible to the responsible division and official. Agency websites and resources such as the *U.S. Government Manual* and the *Federal Regulatory Directory* have the names of major agency officials, but few listings for other staffers. Commercial resources with more detailed information about personnel, such as telephone numbers and e-mail addresses, include *Carroll's Federal Directory* (www.carrollpublishing.com) and Leadership Directories' *Federal Yellow Book* (www.leadershipdirectories.com). Both publishers also produce companion volumes covering federal regional offices outside the Washington, D.C. area.

§ 6–3.   Federal Regulations

The basic mechanism by which most agencies govern is the *regulation*, a detailed administrative order similar in form to a statute. Regulations are also known as *rules*, and these terms are used interchangeably in U.S. administrative law. The publication of regulations follows a standard procedure: they are first issued chronologically in a daily gazette, the *Federal Register*; and then the rules in force are arranged by subject in the *Code of Federal Regulations* (*CFR*). This publication of regulations, first chronologically and then by topic, mirrors the way statutes are published in the *Statutes at Large* and the *United States Code*.

a. Federal Register

As the federal government promulgated more and more executive and administrative orders in the early New Deal period, locating regulations and determining which were in force became increasingly difficult. There was no requirement that regulations be published or centrally filed. Two cases even reached the U.S. Supreme Court before it was discovered that the administrative orders on which they were based were no longer in effect. The resulting criticism led Congress to establish a daily publication of executive and administrative promulgations, the *Federal Register*, the first issue of which appeared in March 1936.

The Administrative Procedure Act in 1946 expanded the scope of the *Federal Register* by creating a rulemaking system requiring the publication of proposed regulations for public comment. Judicial decisions in the 1960s and 1970s overturned regulations seen as arbitrary or capricious and led agencies to give fuller explanations of their actions and greater evidence of public involvement in the decision-making process. Since 1973 agencies have been required to preface final rules with an explanatory preamble, and since 1976 this preamble has included summaries of comments submitted and the agency's responses to these comments.

The introductory preambles appear only in the *Federal Register* and are not reprinted with the text of regulations in the *Code of Federal Regulations*. A *Federal Register* preamble can be invaluable in interpreting the scope and meaning of a regulation in the same way that committee reports and other legislative materials help explain the purpose of a statute. The *Register* may also be the only available source for temporary changes occurring between annual *CFR* revisions.

The *Federal Register* is published in print, but most researchers access the *Register* online. Issues since volume 59 (1994) are available free on the Office of the Federal Register website (www.federal register.gov). A search box at the top of each screen can be used for basic keyword searches and to retrieve material by citation, and an Advanced Search screen allows you to specify agency, type of document, and publication date. Each major agency has its own page on which you can browse recent documents and significant regulations. FDsys (www. gpo.gov/fdsys/) also has issues since 1994, in PDF format.

The *Federal Register* is also available online through several commercial services. Westlaw, Lexis, and Bloomberg Law all have current issues the day they are published, with coverage extending back to the first *Federal Register* issue in 1936. Some older documents are available only in PDF (and may not be full-text searchable), but these materials are usually retrieved by citation anyway. Documents since at least 1981 are fully searchable.

Each daily *Federal Register*, in print or on FDsys, begins with a table of contents and a list of the *Code of Federal Regulations* parts affected by new or proposed regulations in the issue. The table of contents is organized alphabetically by agency, so you can easily monitor a particular agency's activity. Skimming the *Register*'s table of contents is part of many lawyers' daily routine. You can sign up on the Federal Register's site to have the table of contents delivered each morning by e-mail, or set up a more focused custom notification for a particular agency or specific search results. Readers' aids in the back of each issue include a cumulative list of *CFR* parts affected during the current month.

The Office of the Federal Register website has additional information, including tutorials on the rulemaking process and the publication of regulations. An index to the *Federal Register* is published monthly and cumulates over the course of the year. The index is arranged like the daily table of contents, with entries by agency rather than by subject, and is available back to 1936 on HeinOnline.

Lawyers whose clients are subject to federal regulation need to know more than the rules currently in force. They also need to anticipate rule changes and to track developments in pending regulations. A notice of proposed rulemaking (NPRM) can be just as important to a client as a newly adopted regulation. Several tools are available for monitoring the development of regulations that have not yet come into force.

One way to learn about the status of proposed rules and about areas of agency activity that have not even reached the proposed rulemaking stage is through the Unified Agenda of Federal Regulatory and Deregulatory Actions, from the Office of Management and Budget's Office of Information and Regulatory Affairs (www.reginfo.gov). The Unified Agenda lists and summarizes regulatory actions under development and provides information on their projected dates of completion, although those dates are subject to revision. An abridged Unified Agenda of significant rulemaking actions is published twice a year in the *Federal Register*.

Dockets for some regulatory decision-making are available online, providing access to agency analyses, public comments, and other documents involved in the rulemaking process. Regulations.gov (www.regulations.gov) is a centralized site for commenting on proposed regulations and viewing submitted comments.

b. Code of Federal Regulations

As with statutes, chronological publication of regulations is insufficient for most legal research. You must know what regulations are currently in force regardless of when they were first promulgated. The *Code of Federal Regulations* was first published in 1938 to meet this need, and it now consists of more than 230 paperback volumes revised on an annual basis.

The regulations in the *CFR* are collected from the *Federal Register* and arranged in a subject scheme of fifty titles. (Some *CFR* titles cover the same topics as the *U.S. Code* title with the same number, but others focus on completely different subjects.) Titles are divided into chapters, each containing the regulations of a specific agency. Every *CFR* volume includes an alphabetical list of federal agencies indicating the title and chapter (or chapters) of each agency's regulations.

The regulations in a *CFR* chapter are divided into subchapters, each covering a general subject area, and parts, each of which consists of a body of regulations on a particular topic or agency function. Parts are sometimes divided further into subparts, and finally into sections, the basic unit of the code. The citation identifying a *CFR* section shows the title, the part and the section (but not the chapter or subchapter), followed by the year of publication. The section is a distinct number, not a decimal; 9 C.F.R. § 2.131, for example, follows § 2.130 and does not fall between § 2.13 and § 2.14.

At the beginning of each *CFR* part or subpart is an *authority note* showing the statutory authority under which the regulations have been issued. This is followed by a *source note* providing the citation and date of the *Federal Register* in which the regulations were published. The source note is the key to finding the preamble with background information and comments explaining the regulations. If an individual section was added or amended more recently than the other sections in a part, it is followed by a separate source note.

The Bluebook mandates citation to the official, annually revised edition of the *CFR*, available in print and online through FDsys. The official volumes are updated and replaced on a rotating cycle throughout the year. Titles 1–16 have regulations in force as of January 1; titles 17–27 as of April 1; titles 28–41 as of July 1; and titles 42–50 as of October 1. The revised versions are usually available two to four months after these cutoff dates.

In addition to the official *CFR* in PDF, FDsys also offers a much more current Electronic Code of Federal Regulations, or e-CFR (www.ecfr.gov). This edition incorporates new amendments from the *Federal Register* within a day or two. While the site explains that this is not an official legal edition of the *CFR* and is subject to correction, it is a much more useful and timely version of regulations than the annual volume.

Regularly updated versions of the *CFR* are also available online from several commercial sources, including Westlaw, Lexis, and Bloomberg Law. Like the e-CFR, these files are updated on an ongoing basis to reflect changes published in the *Federal Register* and incorporate amendments within days of their appearance in the *Register*. Westlaw even includes red flags indicating an "Adopted Regulation" the same day that an amendment is published.

Older editions of the *CFR* are sometimes needed to identify regulations in force at a particular time. FDsys has coverage starting in mid-1996. Westlaw offers deeper historical access, with older editions of the *CFR* back to 1984. HeinOnline's Code of Federal Regulations Library fills the rest of the gap, covering from the original 1938 edition through the current version.

c. Regulatory Research

Research in federal regulations involves several distinct steps, from finding relevant regulations to searching for documents that might affect their validity. It is always important to verify that regulations are current, and to look for cases in which they are applied and interpreted. You may also need to track changes over time by reading the *Federal Register* or older editions of the *CFR*.

Finding Regulations. You can find federal regulations in several ways. The *Federal Register* and the *Code of Federal Regulations* have indexes, and both publications can be searched through FDsys or other services. Both annotated editions of federal statutes include citations to regulations after code sections. Agency websites have links to regulations, and references are often found in cases, texts, and articles.

Most research into a federal agency's regulations begins with the *Code of Federal Regulations*, rather than the daily *Federal Register*. The current *CFR*, as noted above, is available online from the government and through several services. To find regulations by keyword, it is often most effective to search within a particular title or a specific topical area such as banking, environmental law, or securities. Another approach is to check an agency's website. Most agency sites have their current body of regulations and information on current proposed rules, as well as the texts of the statutes under which they operate.

The *CFR* includes an annually revised *Index and Finding Aids* volume, but its coverage is far less detailed than most statutory indexes. It has only broad references to *CFR* parts, not specific references to individual sections. Much more detailed subject access is provided in the four-volume *West's Code of Federal Regulations General Index*, which is also available on Westlaw.

If you have a statute and need to find regulations promulgated under its authority or related to it, the simplest method is to check the *United States Code Annotated* (in print or on Westlaw) or *United States Code Service* (in print or on Lexis). Cross-references or links to relevant *CFR* parts or sections follow individual sections in both codes.

ProQuest Regulatory Insight (regulatoryinsight. proquest.com) is a new product introduced in late 2015 that collects the *Federal Register* and *CFR* documents related to a particular Public Law, allowing you to examine the implementation of a statutory mandate. Documents are searchable and include both proposed and final rules. Initial coverage is for laws enacted since 2001.

For some agencies, regulations are reprinted in treatises and looseleaf services covering their topical area. Looseleaf services focusing on the work of agencies such as the Internal Revenue Service or the Securities and Exchange Commission have regularly updated and well-annotated texts of both statutes and regulations.

Finding relevant regulations, however, is only the first step of research. You also need to verify that those regulations are current, and find cases and other documents that apply and interpret the regulations.

Updating and Tracking Changes. Making sure that you have the current language of a regulation is a relatively simple task for users of the e-CFR or online services, as these sources are regularly updated with new changes. When using the *CFR* in its print format or in its official version on FDsys, you will need to update a regulation from the most recent annual *CFR* edition.

The simplest course is to check a section in the e-CFR or an online service to see if it lists among its sources any *Federal Register* issues more recent than the latest annual *CFR* revision. Another tool for updating regulations is a monthly pamphlet accompanying the *CFR* (and available on FDsys and HeinOnline) entitled *LSA: List of CFR Sections Affected*, which lists the *Federal Register* pages of any rule changes since the most recent annual revision. The most recent changes can be found by using the cumulative "List of CFR Parts Affected" in the latest *Federal Register* issue.

This somewhat cumbersome process used to be the standard *CFR* updating procedure. While it is no longer required, *LSA* remains a convenient resource for scanning an entire *CFR* chapter to identify recent regulatory changes. You can also use it to track down an older *CFR* reference cited in a case or article. A cited regulation may have been repealed or transferred to another *CFR* location, but *LSA* tables identify the fates of all sections that have been repealed, transferred, or amended.

Interpreting Regulations. The official *CFR*, whether used in print or online (including the e-CFR), contains no annotations of court decisions like those in *United States Code Annotated* or *United States Code Service*. Yet a court may invalidate a regulation or provide an important interpretation of key provisions, and identifying relevant cases is an essential part of regulatory research.

The most convenient way to find court decisions is to use the Westlaw or Lexis version of the *CFR*, which includes notes of decisions similar to those in annotated statutory codes as well as references to relevant agency decisions, statutes, and secondary sources. This in effect gives regulations the same treatment as statutes, providing a springboard from the text to a wide range of research references.

The Westlaw display also includes symbols such as red flags for sections that have been amended, repealed, or adversely affected by court decisions. On Lexis, the Shepard's link offers the "Subsection reports by specific court citation" option that lists references under the particular subsection cited. This can be a great time-saver if you are looking for references to a specific passage within a long, detailed *CFR* provision.

§ 6–4.   Guidance Documents

Regulations published in the *Federal Register* and *CFR* are the most authoritative sources of agency law. Over the years, however, the creation of regulations has become increasingly time-consuming and complicated, as agencies must solicit and consider comments from interested parties. As a result, agencies now are just as likely to create policy through guidance documents, statements, or manuals that do not require notice-and-comment procedures and publication in the *Federal Register*. Although guidance documents do not have the same binding force as regulations, they can be important indicators of how an agency perceives its mandate and how it will respond in a specific situation.

Most guidance documents do not appear in the *Federal Register*, the *CFR*, or any other widely available published source, but they are (or should be) available through agency websites. The Electronic Freedom of Information Act Amendments of 1996 mandates that agencies make policy statements, manuals, and frequently requested information available to the public electronically. Under a 2007 Office of Management and Budget bulletin, agency websites are now required to maintain current lists of significant guidance documents in effect, with links to each document.

Even though guidance documents are important statements of agency policy, there is little consistency in their form and function between agencies. Website organization and ease of access vary considerably from agency to agency. An understanding of guidance documents requires a familiarity with an agency's website and the ways in which the agency informs interested parties of its policies and interpretations.

Agency websites have greatly increased access to government information, but there remains a vast store of additional unpublished documentation such as internal records, correspondence, and staff studies. Under the Freedom of Information Act, individuals can request copies of most documents (although it may take weeks or months to receive a reply and there are broad exceptions for material that agencies need not disclose). The first place to check for policies and procedures is the department or agency's website, which should have a Freedom of Information or FOIA link on its front page.

Several resources are available for assistance in filing FOIA requests. The Reporters Committee for Freedom of the Press has an iFOIA website (www.ifoia.org), which includes a Federal Open Government Guide and a template for filing FOIA requests. The House Committee on Government Reform publishes a concise handbook with sample request forms, *A Citizen's Guide on Using the Freedom of Information Act and the Privacy Act of 1974 to Request Government Records*, H.R. Rep. 112–689 (2012). Procedures and sample forms for filing requests and suing to compel disclosure are also available in P. Stephen Gidiere III, *The Federal Information Manual: How the Government Collects, Manages, and Discloses Information Under FOIA and Other Statutes* (2d ed., 2013).

§ 6–5. Administrative Decisions and Rulings

While regulations and guidance documents are the primary means by which most agencies create legal rules within their areas of expertise, administrative agencies also have quasi-judicial functions in which they hold hearings and issue decisions involving specific parties. Although in most instances decisions and rulings do not have binding authority in later cases, they have considerable precedential value for attorneys practicing before an agency or appealing an agency decision.

Formal Adjudications. Agency hearings are usually conducted by an administrative law judge, whose decision can be appealed to a higher authority, usually within the agency. Review of a final agency decision can generally be sought in federal court.

About fifteen regulatory commissions and other agencies publish their decisions in a form similar to official reports of court decisions. These reports, listed in Table 1.2 in *The Bluebook*, are the sources to which decisions should be cited if they appear therein. HeinOnline and LLMC Digital have comprehensive PDF collections of published reports. Recent decisions are also available from agency websites, but coverage and search options vary widely.

Westlaw and Lexis include decisions of more than seventy agencies and offices in topical databases. They have many administrative decisions not published in official reports, and coverage generally

extends much earlier than official websites. Bloomberg Law also has decisions and other documents
from numerous agencies, with coverage for some
sources that is broader than what is available on the
official websites.

Many administrative decisions are also published,
along with other documents such as statutes,
regulations, and court decisions, in topical looseleaf
services. These services, which usually combine
access to primary sources with commentary and
current information, will be discussed in Chapter 8.

A researcher specializing in a particular area must
be familiar with decisions of relevant agencies.
Nonspecialists can learn about administrative
decisions that interpret a particular statute from the
notes of decisions in *United States Code Service* (in
print or on Lexis), which includes coverage of more
than fifty commissions and boards. *United States
Code Annotated* (in print or on Westlaw) does not
have summaries of administrative decisions, but the
Citing References display for a *USCA* section
includes an Administrative Decisions & Guidance
section listing relevant documents. On either
Westlaw or Lexis, you can also trace references that
cite an administrative decision to find later
documents that may affect its validity or aid in
interpretation.

Advice Letters and Other Rulings. Agencies
also issue advice to individuals or businesses seeking
clarification of policies or regulations as applied to
particular factual situations. This advice is usually
accompanied by a disclaimer that the reply has no

precedential value in future instances, but it is nonetheless a strong indication of how an agency will interpret its governing law.

Internal Revenue Service private letter rulings and Securities and Exchange Commission no-action letters are leading examples of these types of agency documents. These communications were originally sent only to the recipients and not made public, but changing views of the value of informal rulings led to their availability in print and online.

Materials like private letter rulings and no-action letters are generally available from agency websites and in printed looseleaf services, as well as from commercial services. Westlaw, Lexis, and Bloomberg Law offer sophisticated search options and combine these materials with other relevant materials from the agencies and courts.

The difficult first step is identifying what informal documentation is available from a particular agency. This can be done by perusing its website, by noting the sources cited in the case law and secondary literature, or by studying a guide to the resources in a particular area of law.

Attorney General Opinions. As the federal government's law firm, the Department of Justice provides legal advice to the president and to other departments. These opinions are advisory and not binding, but they are usually given some persuasive authority. Until 1977, opinions were signed by the U.S. Attorney General and published in a series entitled *Opinions of the Attorneys General of the*

United States. This function is now delegated to the Office of Legal Counsel (OLC), which has published *Opinions of the Office of Legal Counsel* since 1977. Opinions of the Attorney General and OLC are available online through the major commercial services, including HeinOnline, with coverage back to 1791, and OLC opinions since 1992 are on its website (www.justice.gov/olc/).

§ 6–6. Presidential Lawmaking

The president has the power to veto legislation passed by Congress and the duty to enforce enacted laws, and supervises the workings of the departments and administrative agencies. The president also has a wide-ranging lawmaking authority in his or her own right, as the nation's agent of foreign relations and its military commander. In fulfilling these roles and functions, the president issues executive orders, proclamations, and other documents of legal effect.

Background information on the presidency is available in numerous sources. Two of the more comprehensive reference works are *Encyclopedia of the American Presidency* (Leonard W. Levy & Louis Fisher eds., 1994) and *Guide to the Presidency and the Executive Branch* (Michael Nelson ed., 5th ed. 2013). Presidential lawmaking is the focus of Louis Fisher, *The Law of the Executive Branch: Presidential Power* (2014).

a. Executive Orders and Proclamations

The major legal documents issued by the president are *executive orders* and *proclamations*. Executive orders usually involve an exercise of presidential authority related to government business, while proclamations are announcements of policy or of matters requiring public notice. Proclamations are often ceremonial or commemorative, but some have important legal effects such as implementing trade agreements or declaring treaties to be in force.

Executive orders and proclamations are issued in separate numbered series and published in the *Federal Register*. They are available, with other *Register* materials, from FDsys since 1994. Westlaw has executive orders since 1936 and other presidential documents since 1984, and Lexis has executive orders since 1980.

The most comprehensive retrospective source for these documents is ProQuest Executive Orders and Presidential Proclamations 1789–2014, available as a component of ProQuest Congressional. This collection includes PDFs of numerous historic orders, many of them unnumbered, before the beginning of *Federal Register* and *CFR* publication. The American Presidency Project at the University of California, Santa Barbara (www.presidency.ucsb.edu) has free online access to executive orders dating back to 1826 and proclamations back to 1789, but it does not include the *CFR* or *Federal Register* references needed for citations.

Executive orders and proclamations are reprinted in a number of locations, including an annual compilation of Title 3 of the *Code of Federal Regulations*. Because each annual edition of Title 3 is a unique set of documents rather than an updated codification, older volumes remain part of the current *CFR* set. Documents from the years 1936 to 1975 have been recompiled into multiyear hardcover editions, and all volumes since 1936 are available online through HeinOnline. The *CFR* is the preferred *Bluebook* source for the presidential documents it contains.

Proclamations, but not executive orders, are printed in the annual *Statutes at Large* volumes. Major orders and proclamations are also reprinted in the notes following related statutory provisions in the *U.S. Code*, *USCA*, and *USCS*. The *U.S. Code* is an important source, if only because *The Bluebook* requires a parallel U.S.C. citation if available. Tables in each version of the code list presidential documents by number and indicate where they can be found.

Westlaw and Lexis also note citations to proclamations and executive orders, and the National Archives maintains disposition tables of all executive orders since 1937 (www.archives.gov/federal-register/executive-orders/) with information on amendment, revocation, and current status.

b. *Other Presidential Documents*

The president issues several other documents with legal significance. These include various memoranda, reports, speeches, and messages to Congress.

Memoranda and Directives. A variety of other documents are printed in the *Federal Register* along with executive orders and proclamations, but are not included as part of either series. Presidential determinations pursuant to specific statutory mandates are issued in a numbered series, and unnumbered documents include memoranda and notices. Many of these deal with foreign affairs and homeland security. These documents are reprinted in the annual cumulation of 3 C.F.R. in a separate section following executive orders.

Some presidential directives relating to national security issues are not published in the *Federal Register* or *CFR*. The Federal Register Act requires only that proclamations and executive orders be published, so other documents can be used to advance presidential goals in greater secret. These have a variety of names such as Homeland Security Presidential Directives or Presidential Policy Directives. These directives are often not easy to obtain, but a Federation of American Scientists website (fas.org/irp/offdocs/direct.htm) lists the designations and directives used by presidents since Truman and has links to many of the documents.

Reorganization Plans. A reorganization plan consisting of a presidential proposal to transfer or abolish agency functions was a mechanism used from

1946 to 1979. Several major agencies, including the Environmental Protection Agency, were initially created by reorganization plans, and the plan may still be relevant in interpreting the scope of an agency's powers. These plans were published in the *Federal Register*, *CFR*, and *Statutes at Large*, and many are reprinted in the *U.S. Code*.

Messages to Congress. Communications to Congress by the president may propose new legislation, explain vetoes, transmit reports or other documents, or convey information about the state of national affairs or some other matter of concern. Messages are published in the *Congressional Record* and as House Documents. Messages proposing legislation may have some value in determining the intent of laws that are enacted as a result.

The messages or statements issued when the President signs or vetoes particular enactments can also shed light on legislative history. Presidents sometimes use signing statements to convey interpretations of ambiguous or controversial provisions. These statements have been included in *USCCAN*'s legislative history section beginning in 1986, although their importance in interpreting statutory language is subject to dispute.

Compilations of Presidential Papers. The most comprehensive source for current presidential material is the *Daily Compilation of Presidential Documents*, which succeeded the *Weekly Compilation of Presidential Documents* in January 2009. The *Daily Compilation* includes nominations, announcements, and transcripts of speeches and press conferences, as well as executive orders, proclamations, signing statements, and other legally significant documents. *Daily Compilation* and *Weekly Compilation* issues are available in PDF on FDsys back to 1993, and HeinOnline has comprehensive coverage back to the first *Weekly Compilation* volume in 1965. Westlaw coverage begins in 2000.

Public Papers of the Presidents is an official series of annual volumes compiling presidential documents. Volumes have been published for Herbert Hoover and for all presidents after Franklin D. Roosevelt, and the papers of Roosevelt and most earlier presidents are generally available in commercially published editions. FDsys provides access to *Public Papers* volumes beginning with 1991, and searchable retrospective collections of the entire set and earlier compilations are available from HeinOnline and the American Presidency Project.

§ 6–7.   State Administrative Law

Like the federal government, the states have experienced a dramatic increase in the number and activity of their administrative agencies. In most states, however, publication of agency rules and decisions is less systematic than it is on the federal level.

a. Websites and Directories

State websites are often the best starting point to determine the jurisdiction of relevant agencies and their publications, and many have directories with contact information for government officials. If a search engine does not quickly lead you to the state homepage, numerous websites including the Library of Congress (www.loc.gov/rr/news/stategov/) have links for each state.

Nearly all states publish official manuals paralleling the *United States Government Manual* and providing quick access to information about government agencies and officials. Some of these directories describe state agency functions and publications, while others simply serve as government phone directories. They are described in the annual *State Legislative Sourcebook*, along with information about reference works, statistical abstracts, and other sources. The American Library Association's "State Blue Books and Encyclopedias" (wikis.ala.org/godort/index.php?title=State_Blue_Books_and_Encyclopedias) has links to online versions.

A number of directories have multistate access to officials' names and contact information. *Carroll's State Directory* (www.carrollpublishing.com) and Leadership Directories' *State Yellow Book* (www.leadershipdirectories.com) have detailed coverage. The Council of State Governments' *CSG State Directory* lists officials by function, rather than by state, and may be most convenient for someone needing to contact similar officials in several states. CSG's annual *Book of the States* (knowledgecenter.csg.org) supplements these directories with more than 170 tables presenting a broad range of information on government operations in each of the fifty states.

b. Regulations and Executive Orders

Almost every state issues a subject compilation of its administrative regulations, similar to the *C.F.R.*, and most supplement these with weekly, biweekly, or monthly registers.

Almost every state makes its administrative code and register available on its government website. One of the easiest ways to find these sources is through the National Association of Secretaries of State's list, Administrative Rules Online by State (www.administrativerules.org). The commercial services also have administrative codes from each state, and Westlaw has "50 State Regulatory Surveys" with citations and links for each state's administrative code provisions on several hundred topics.

The Bluebook and *ALWD Guide* identify administrative codes and registers in their lists of basic primary sources for each state. More detailed information is available in William H. Manz, *Guide to State Legislation, Legislative History, and Administrative Materials* (7th ed. 2008, available in HeinOnline), which lists print and online sources for each state's administrative code.

Some of the administrative codes and registers include executive orders or similar legal pronouncements from governors. Several governors include executive orders on their websites, which can be accessed through state government homepages or by links from the National Governors Association (www.nga.org). Sources for executive orders are also listed in *Guide to State Legislation, Legislative History, and Administrative Materials.*

c. Decisions, Rulings, and Other Documents

Decisions of some state agencies, especially those dealing with banking, insurance, public utilities, taxation, and workers' compensation, may be published in official form in chronological series. A few looseleaf services and topical reporters also include state administrative decisions, and a growing number of state agency decisions are included in the online services and on agency websites. *Guide to State Legislation, Legislative History, and Administrative Materials* lists publications and online sources for agency rulings, decisions, and orders.

State attorney general opinions, issued in response to questions from government officials, can have considerable significance in legal research. Although attorney general opinions are advisory and have no binding authority, they are given considerable weight by the courts in interpreting statutes and regulations. Most states publish attorney general opinions in bound volumes. Many attorneys general also have recent opinions on their websites, which can be found through links at the National Association of Attorneys General website (www. naag.org). State attorney general opinions are available in Westlaw and Lexis, with coverage in most states beginning in 1977 or earlier; Bloomberg Law has more recent opinions from selected states. Some attorney general opinions are included in the annotations in state codes, but coverage varies from state to state. Westlaw also includes attorney general opinions as citing sources in its coverage of cases, statutes, and other sources. If you are working from an attorney general opinion, however, citing references are not listed so you would need to search by keyword to track its treatment in cases and articles.

As with federal agencies, guidance documents and other publications from agencies can also be important in interpreting state law. Materials such as guidelines and manuals increasingly are available from agency websites.

Like the federal government, each state has open records laws under which unpublished information can be obtained upon request. The National Freedom of Information Coalition (www.nfoic.org/state-foi-resources) and the Reporters Committee for Freedom of the Press's Open Government Guide (rcfp.org/open-government-guide) have information on each state's laws and procedures.

§ 6–8.　Local Law

Legal problems and issues are governed by the laws of counties, cities, and other local units, in addition to federal and state law. Housing, transportation, social welfare, education, municipal services, zoning, and environmental conditions are all heavily regulated at the local level of government.

Cities and counties are administrative units of the states, with lawmaking powers determined by state constitution or by legislative delegation of authority. They create a variety of legal documents that can be important in legal research. *Charters* are the basic laws creating the structure of local government, and *ordinances* are local enactments governing specific issues. In addition many localities have administrative agencies that issue rules or decisions.

Most county and city codes, especially in larger jurisdictions, are available online. State and Local Government on the Net (www.statelocalgov.net) can lead you to county and city homepages, which provide background and contact information if not the text of ordinances. Two of the leading publishers of local codes, both of which offer free online access, are American Legal Publishing Corp. (www.amlegal. com) and Municipal Code Corporation (www. municode.com).

State and local law often incorporates industry codes on areas such as construction and fire safety. The International Code Council (www.iccsafe.org) publishes a series of fourteen codes on building standards and related issues, and the Building Codes Resource Center (www.reedconstructiondata.com/ building-codes/) identifies the codes in force in specific states and major cities. PDF versions of many of these codes are available from Public.Resource.org (law.resource.org/pub/us/code/safety.html).

Because much local law information is not available in print or on the Internet, direct contact by telephone or e-mail may be essential. Directories with information on local governments throughout the country include *Carroll's County Directory*,

Carroll's Municipal Directory, and *Municipal Yellow Book*, all available in print and online.

CHAPTER 7

COURT RULES AND PRACTICE

Images of some resources discussed in this chapter are at **libguides.law.virginia.edu/nutshell12/ch7**

---

§ 7–1.   Introduction

This chapter discusses a number of resources dealing with court proceedings and legal practice. Some, such as the rules governing trial procedures and lawyer conduct, are primary legal sources. Briefs and docket sheets contain background information on decided cases or pending lawsuits. Directories and formbooks provide practical assistance for anyone who needs to contact courts, draft documents, or transact other legal business.

Litigators need to be familiar with these materials, but their value also extends to other legal research situations. All lawyers must follow rules of professional conduct, and resources such as briefs and model jury instructions can be useful sources of information about substantive legal issues.

§ 7–2. Court Rules

Rules regulating court proceedings have the force of law, but they generally cannot supersede or conflict with statutes. Most jurisdictions have sets of rules governing trial and appellate procedure, as well as rules for specialized tribunals or for particular actions such as admiralty or habeas corpus. Some of these rules are enacted by statute, but most are promulgated by the courts themselves or by conferences of judges.

a. Federal Rules

Under the Rules Enabling Act, 28 U.S.C. § 2072, federal courts have the power to adopt rules governing their procedures as long as they do not "abridge, enlarge, or modify any substantive right."

Rules of National Scope. Individual federal courts have had rules since the beginning of the judicial system, but the modern era of rulemaking began with the adoption of the Federal Rules of Civil Procedure in 1938. These were prepared by a judicial advisory committee and approved by the Supreme Court, as were subsequent sets of rules governing criminal procedure (1946) and appellate procedure (1968). The Federal Rules of Evidence were originally drafted by judges, but they were enacted by Congress in 1975 due to concerns about their potential impact on substantive rights.

These rules governing federal court proceedings can be found in online and print sources, some unannotated and others accompanied by advisory committee notes, summaries of judicial decisions, and extensive commentaries. Each of the major sets of rules is printed in the *United States Code*, accompanied by its advisory committee's explanatory comments after each section. These comments discuss procedure under prior law and the purpose of the new rule or amendment, and are often an invaluable starting point in interpreting a rule provision. *United States Code Annotated* (*USCA*) (in print and on Westlaw) and *United States Code Service* (*USCS*) (in print and on Lexis) also include annotations of cases in which the rules have been applied or construed, as well as references to treatises, law review articles, and legal encyclopedias. These annotations can be copious; the Federal Rules of Civil Procedure, for example, occupy seventeen volumes in *USCA*.

You can find in-depth scholarly analysis of the federal rules in two major treatises, Wright & Miller's *Federal Practice and Procedure* (1st–4th eds. 1969–date, on Westlaw) and *Moore's Federal Practice* (3d ed. 1997–date, on Lexis). These treatises are among the secondary sources most often cited by the federal courts. They are organized rule-by-rule, with the texts and official comments accompanied by historical background and detailed discussion of cases. Both analyze the civil, criminal, and appellate rules, as well as jurisdictional issues such as venue and *res judicata*; *Federal Practice and Procedure* also covers the Federal Rules of Evidence. *Weinstein's*

Federal Evidence (2d ed. 1997–date, on Lexis) has similar rule-by-rule treatment of the Federal Rules of Evidence.

Most court rules are available at free websites, but usually without the helpful commentary and annotations found in the treatises and annotated codes. The House Committee on the Judiciary website has PDF documents of each of the major sets of rules (judiciary.house.gov/index.cfm/procedural-documents). The Administrative Office of the U.S. Courts website has a section on Federal Rulemaking (www.uscourts.gov/rules-policies), with links to these sources as well as information on recent and proposed amendments. The Legal Information Institute has searchable versions of the federal rules (www.law.cornell.edu/rules/).

Local Rules. Individual courts also have local rules to supplement the national sets of rules. Local court rules often govern procedural matters such as the format of documents and the time allowed to file papers. Over the years, however, they have proliferated into an array of local requirements that has been called a "balkanization" of federal procedure. In addition to rules for each district, individual judges can also promulgate guidelines for the cases they hear. Litigators must be every bit as aware of local and judge-specific rules as they are of more general rules.

The E-Government Act of 2002 requires that each court's website include its local rules and individual judges' rules. Many court websites also have answers to frequently asked questions about filing requirements and trial procedures. Links to local court homepages are available through the Administrative Office of the U.S. Courts website (www.uscourts.gov/court-locator).

The U.S. Supreme Court's rules are available on its website (www.supremecourt.gov) and are also included in the *U.S. Code*, *USCA*, and *USCS*. The rules for each of the Courts of Appeals are also published in *USCA* and *USCS*, with annotations of court decisions applying the rules.

Local court rules are also available from the major online services, linked to any citing cases and other documents. U.S. District Court rules are usually available in court rules pamphlets published for individual states, some of which include annotations. Court of Appeals and District Court rules from the entire country are published, unannotated, in a ten-volume looseleaf set, *Federal Local Court Rules* (4th ed. 2013–date). Rules of individual judges are published in the three-volume *Directory of Federal Court Guidelines* (1996–date, available on Westlaw).

Sentencing Guidelines. The Federal Sentencing Guidelines are not court rules, but they occupy a similar position in the hierarchy of legal authorities. Judges must consider the guidelines in determining punishments for criminal convictions. The U.S. Sentencing Commission, an independent agency within the judicial branch, first promulgated the guidelines in 1987 and has revised them numerous times. The commission publishes its *Guidelines Manual* online (www.ussc.gov) and in print.

The sentencing guidelines are not included in the official *U.S. Code*, but both *USCA* (on Westlaw) and *USCS* (on Lexis) have annotated versions of the guidelines with notes of court decisions and citing references.

Federal Practice and Procedure and *Moore's Federal Practice* do not discuss sentencing guidelines, but shorter works such as David Debold et al., *Practice Under the Federal Sentencing Guidelines* (5th ed. 2010–date), and Thomas W. Hutchison et al., *Federal Sentencing Law and Practice* (annual), have similar treatment, with commentary and notes of court decisions applying the guidelines. Both of these are available on Westlaw.

b. *State Rules*

Rules and procedures differ from state to state. Even though distinctions have decreased somewhat in recent decades as many states have adopted provisions modeled on the federal rules, they remain significant and knowing how to locate local procedures is critical.

Generally, a combination of statutory provisions and court rules govern procedures in state courts. The court rules are usually included in the annotated state codes (in print or on Westlaw or Lexis), accompanied by notes of relevant cases and lists of citations in court decisions, law reviews, and other sources.

State court websites generally include rules and other procedural information. The National Center for State Courts' "Court Web Sites" (www.ncsc.org/

Information-and-Resources/) is one of several directories of trial and appellate state court sites.

Most states also have annual paperback volumes with rules and procedural statutes. More extensive works in larger jurisdictions, such as *Witkin's California Practice* or *Carmody-Wait 2d Cyclopedia of New York Practice* (both available on Westlaw), have scholarly commentaries on the rules and analysis of relevant case law. The state legal research guides listed in Appendix A on pages 291–302 can tell you about these and other jurisdiction-specific resources.

§ 7–3. Legal Ethics

The professional activities of lawyers are generally controlled by the courts, although in some states supervision is delegated to bar associations or oversight boards. The primary sources governing legal ethics are rules of conduct, ethics opinions, and disciplinary decisions. Ethics opinions are advisory documents, usually issued by bar associations, analyzing how lawyers or judges should handle particular or hypothetical problems. Disciplinary decisions punish specific acts of misconduct.

Although provisions and amendments vary from state to state, every jurisdiction but one has adopted some form of the American Bar Association's Model Rules of Professional Conduct. (California, the last holdout, is in the process of considering a proposed revision modeled on the Model Rules.) Each jurisdiction's rules of professional conduct are available online from either the state court system or the state bar. The ABA Center for Professional Responsibility has links to these sites for each state (www.americanbar.org/groups/professional_responsibility/resources/links_of_interest.html).

The rules are also available from the online services and are published in the volumes of state court rules. Only a few of these sources are annotated with notes of decisions under the rules. Unannotated versions of the rules for every state are also available in the looseleaf publication *National Reporter on Legal Ethics and Professional Responsibility*.

Annotated Model Rules of Professional Conduct (8th ed. 2015, available on Westlaw) has the text of the ABA rules with comments, legal background, and notes of decisions from various jurisdictions. This is a useful source for comparative analysis and commentary, even though it does not contain the rules as adopted in any specific state. The American Law Institute has also formulated basic rules of legal ethics in its *Restatement of the Law: The Law Governing Lawyers* (2000, available on both Westlaw and Lexis).

As in other areas of law, you may want to begin your research by consulting a treatise. The leading modern works are Geoffrey C. Hazard, Jr. & W. William Hodes, *The Law of Lawyering* (3d ed. 2000–date), a two-volume set designed as a workbook "for lawyers faced with immediate practical dilemmas," and Ronald D. Rotunda & John S. Dzienkowski, *Legal Ethics: The Lawyer's Deskbook on Professional Responsibility* (annual, available on Westlaw). The *ABA/BNA Lawyers' Manual on Professional Conduct* (available on Bloomberg Law) can also be a good place to start your research. This looseleaf service includes a treatise-like commentary with background and practical tips, as well as news of developments and abstracts of new decisions.

Ethics opinions, generally prepared in response to inquiries from attorneys, are issued by the American Bar Association and by state and local bar associations. ABA opinions are available on Westlaw and Lexis, as are opinions from selected state and local bars. Ethics opinions from 1981 to 2011 can also be found in the *National Reporter on Legal Ethics and Professional Responsibility*, and most state bars either summarize their opinions or publish them in full on their websites.

Judges are governed by rules based in most jurisdictions on the ABA's Model Code of Judicial Conduct. The Model Code and links to state versions are available on the ABA Center for Professional Responsibility's website, and the state rules can also be found in court rules pamphlets. The ABA has published an *Annotated Model Code of Judicial Conduct* (2d ed. 2011), and Charles Gardner Geyh et al., *Judicial Conduct and Ethics* (5th ed. 2013, available on Lexis) analyzes issues in this area.

§ 7–4.   Briefs and Other Court Documents

You can learn a great deal about a case by reviewing the materials submitted to the court by the parties. For appellate cases, two types of documents are particularly informative. *Briefs* are the written arguments and authorities cited by the attorneys for the parties. *Records* are documents from the lower court proceeding submitted as an appendix to the briefs, and include pleadings, motions, trial transcripts, and judgments. Some appellate cases also have petitions for review (such as the *petitions for certiorari* or *statements of probable jurisdiction* in the Supreme Court) and various motions. The progress of cases at the trial level is far less systematic, and the documents produced vary widely from case to case.

In either trial or appellate court, a case generally begins with an initial filing such as a complaint or appeal. It is then assigned a *case number* or *docket number*, which is used to identify the case and its documents. A docket generally lists the parties, their attorneys, and each action in the case in chronological order. The docket number is the key to finding case documents, and is usually given at the beginning of a published decision.

Supreme Court Briefs. As you might expect, the most widely available briefs are those filed in United States Supreme Court cases. Supreme Court case files are often quite voluminous, as many cases have not only the parties' briefs but also numerous filings by *amici curiae* ("friends of the court") supporting one side or the other.

Most Supreme Court briefs are now available online. The American Bar Association website has briefs in cases decided on the merits since 2003 and scheduled for oral argument (www.americanbar.org/publications/preview_home.html). Its coverage of *amicus* briefs begins in 2007. Filings by parties and *amici* back to the 1930s (with only selective coverage before the late 1970s) are available through Westlaw, Lexis, and Bloomberg Law. Retrospective online coverage is offered by Thomson Gale's The Making of Modern Law: U.S. Supreme Court Records and Briefs, 1832–1978 (gdc.gale.com).

Briefs for hundreds of major cases, dating back to the 19th century, are reprinted in *Landmark Briefs and Arguments of the Supreme Court of the United States: Constitutional Law*. Recent briefs are more conveniently available online, but *Landmark Briefs* is very useful for its coverage of cases through the 1973 term in the first eighty volumes of the set.

Supreme Court Oral Arguments. Transcripts of Supreme Court oral arguments are also available in various formats. The Supreme Court website has current PDF transcripts within hours of argument, as well as older arguments beginning with the 2000 term. Online coverage starts in 1979 on Lexis and in 1990 on Westlaw, and microform collections begin with the 1953 term. Arguments in major cases are available in *Landmark Briefs and Arguments of the Supreme Court of the United States: Constitutional Law*. The Oyez Project (www.oyez.org) has several thousand hours of recorded audio for arguments dating back to 1955.

If full argument transcripts are unavailable for a case, you may find excerpts in contemporary newspaper accounts. One of the most thorough sources for information on arguments since the 1930s is *The United States Law Week* (uslw.bna.com), BNA's weekly newsletter on the Court's activities. It reports in detail on several dozen arguments each term.

One way to determine the status of a Supreme Court case or to identify documents is through the Court's website, which has information on cases pending on the docket, schedules of upcoming oral arguments, and other information.

The United States Law Week also has information on the Supreme Court's docket, with a record of proceedings and summaries of cases filed. Online, the Supreme Court Today section of the website provides several ways to track Supreme Court cases and is regularly updated with new decisions, filings, and other developments. In print, *Law Week*'s Supreme Court binder includes summaries of cases, the journal of the Court's proceedings, an index by topic and case name, and a table listing cases by docket number with references to developments.

Other Appellate Courts. Records and briefs of the U.S. Courts of Appeals and state appellate courts are not quite as readily available as those from the U.S. Supreme Court. For federal courts, PACER (Public Access to Court Electronic Records) has docket information, briefs, and other documents in recent cases. Cases are searchable by docket number or by parties' or attorneys' names. Each court has its own PACER or CM/ECF (Case Management/ Electronic Case Files) site, but the system has a centralized registration process (www.pacer.gov), with a nationwide Case Locator that links directly to the docket sheets on individual courts' sites.

There are alternative approaches to PACER dockets and documents, easier and more flexible than the official interface. PacerPro (www.pacerpro.com) is a gateway to PACER with a more modern interface and improved searching options. Bloomberg Law has a Litigation & Dockets tab allowing you to search PACER's information, to update dockets, and to retrieve documents. The full text of documents that have been downloaded through Bloomberg is searchable, making it easy to search for particular motions or arguments.

Online access to filings in state appellate courts is less widespread than it is for federal courts, although a growing number of state court websites now include briefs. Sites for briefs are listed in Michael Whiteman, *Free and Fee-Based Appellate Court Briefs Online* (iti.bz/os111213).

Westlaw has nationwide coverage of federal and state appellate court briefs, back to the 1970s for some federal circuits and more recent for most state courts. (Click on the *i* icon to check the scope of coverage for a specific jurisdiction.) Lexis also has briefs and other filings in its "Briefs and Pleadings" tab, and Bloomberg Law provides access to PACER's docket information and briefs.

Some briefs are available online from non-court websites. Several organizations and government agencies post briefs they have filed in the Supreme Court and in other appellate courts. The U.S. Department of Justice site has Supreme Court briefs filed by the Solicitor General since 1982 (www.justice.gov/

osg/). High profile documents are often available from news sites such as CNN (www.cnn.com).

For most courts, appellate records and briefs can also be found in local law libraries within the circuit or state. In some instances, however, you may need to contact the court or a judicial records center to obtain copies.

Trial Courts. Appellate cases generally follow a standard path and produce specific documents such as the parties' briefs, the lower court record, and the court's opinion. Material from trial court litigation, on the other hand, is more varied and can be harder to identify and find. Some cases result in judges' opinions, such as a decision granting a motion for summary judgment, but many matters are decided without a written opinion. Cases can be decided by jury verdict, summary disposition, or settlement agreement. Some litigation produces dozens of memoranda or briefs submitted to support or oppose motions before, during and after trial, while other cases go to trial without any written submissions on points of law. Trial transcripts, if available, can be voluminous and expensive but may be essential sources of information.

Docket sheets for trial courts increasingly are available online, particularly for federal courts, with a growing number of courts providing online access to documents as well. The federal courts' PACER system covers recent cases in the federal district and bankruptcy courts. While docket sheets and court filings for some state courts are available online, for others this information may be more difficult to obtain. Most states have electronic docket systems, but means of access vary.

As noted earlier, PACER information is also available through Bloomberg Law. You can update a docket to retrieve current information from PACER, obtain any documents that are available electronically, and track a docket to receive notifications of new filings. Westlaw also has PACER dockets and updating capabilities, but filings are not available under academic subscriptions. All three services (Westlaw, Bloomberg Law, and Lexis) have access to docket information and some documents for some state courts.

If electronic access is unavailable, you may need to contact the court directly to obtain a copy of a transcript or other documents. Access methods for both federal and state courts are explained at sites such as Court Reference (www.courtreference.com) and Records Project (recordsproject.com).

Records Project and other sites such as SearchSystems.net also explain how to obtain other public records, such as property and licensing information, much of which is available through state and local government websites. "Public Records" is a link on Westlaw's main screen (except for academic subscriptions), and is an option on the "Research" pull-down menu at the top left of the Lexis display. Both services have real property records, people locators, professional licenses, motor vehicle records, and other information.

Information on trial verdicts and damage awards, primarily for various types of tort litigation, is available in services known as *verdict reporters.* These generally have a brief summary of the case's facts and claims, list attorneys and expert witnesses for each side, and report the resulting verdict. In the absence of any published opinions, this may be the best available record of a case's background and outcome. Westlaw and Lexis both have "Jury Verdicts and Settlements" collections covering federal and state courts.

§ 7–5.   Directories of Courts and Judges

Court directories serve a number of purposes. They have contact information for clerks' offices, and some include judges' biographical data. This can be useful information for litigants appearing before a particular judge or panel, and for law students applying for clerkships after graduation.

Court websites, which usually include judges' contact data as well as some brief biographical information, are easily located by search. Links to sites are accessible through portals such as the Court Locator on the U.S. Courts website (www.uscourts. gov/court-locator) and the list of court sites from the National Center for State Courts (www.ncsc.org).

Almanac of the Federal Judiciary, a two-volume looseleaf publication (available on Westlaw), is the most thorough source for biographical information of federal judges, and includes summaries of noteworthy rulings, media coverage, and lawyers' evaluations of judges' abilities and temperaments.

Several directories cover both federal and state courts. Leadership Directories' *Judicial Yellow Book* (www.leadershipdirectories.com) has basic biographies of judges, as well as listings of court personnel such as clerks and staff attorneys; for the states, it covers appellate courts but not trial courts. CQ's *Federal-State Court Directory* has limited coverage of state courts, but includes charts of each state's court structure. *The American Bench* has biographical information for both federal and state judges; it is arranged by state with an alphabetical name index.

More thorough coverage of state courts is available in *BNA's Directory of State and Federal Courts, Judges, and Clerks* (available on Bloomberg Law) and *Directory of State Court Clerks & County Courthouses*. Tribal courts are covered in *United States Tribal Courts Directory* (4th ed. 2011, available in HeinOnline).

You may sometimes need information about a judge who was involved in an older case or who sat on a particular court. If you know only the last name at the head of an opinion, your first step may be to determine the judge's full name. This can be found in tables in the front of most reporter volumes. For example, since 1882 the *Federal Reporter* has listed the sitting federal judges, with footnotes indicating any changes since the previous volume. Similar listings appear in each of West's regional reporters and in most official state reports. The Federal Judicial Center website (www.fjc.gov) has a database with biographical information about all life-tenured federal judges since 1789. Entries include links to information about manuscript sources and lists of other biographical sources, if available.

§ 7–6.   Forms and Jury Instructions

In the course of legal practice, many basic transactions and court filings occur regularly. Rather than redraft these documents each time, attorneys frequently work from sample versions of standard legal documents and instruments. Model forms are available both online and in print. Some sets of forms are annotated with discussion of the underlying laws, checklists of procedural steps, and citations to relevant cases.

Several multivolume compilations of forms are published. Two of the major national sets are adjuncts to *American Jurisprudence 2d* and are linked to the encyclopedia by frequent cross-references. *Am. Jur. Legal Forms 2d* has transactional instruments such as contracts, leases, and wills, and *Am. Jur. Pleading and Practice Forms* focuses on litigation and other practice before courts and administrative agencies. Both sets are divided into several hundred topical chapters mirroring the organization of *Am. Jur. 2d*, and are available on Westlaw along with the encyclopedia. *West's Legal Forms*, also on Westlaw, is arranged by broad practice areas such as estate planning or real estate, and may be better for reviewing a range of related issues than for finding forms on very fact-specific topics.

Three major sets are devoted to forms used in federal practice, each with a different structure. *Bender's Federal Practice Forms* (on Lexis) is arranged by court rule. *Federal Procedural Forms, Lawyers' Edition* (on Westlaw) is a companion to West's encyclopedic *Federal Procedure, Lawyers' Edition*, and has several dozen subject chapters. *West's Federal Forms* (on Westlaw) is arranged by court, with separate volumes covering forms needed in the Supreme Court, Courts of Appeals, District Courts, Bankruptcy Courts, the Tax Court, and other specialized courts.

Sets of forms are also published for most states and for particular subject areas. Some sets, such as *Bender's Forms of Discovery* (on Lexis), are geared toward specific stages of litigation. Practice-oriented treatises and manuals frequently include appendices of sample forms, and in some states compilations of official forms are issued in conjunction with statutory codes. A source for a specific jurisdiction is usually the best place to start, as it is most likely to conform to the jurisdiction's laws and procedures.

Results from a global search on the main Westlaw or Lexis screen can be filtered to display only forms, then narrowed further by jurisdiction or topic. Alternatively, you can use the Form Finder directory on Westlaw to search all forms or to select a more specific source.

Most jurisdictions have published sets of *model* or *pattern jury instructions*, used by judges to explain the applicable law to jurors. Model jury instructions are useful in research because they provide a concise summary of a jurisdiction's law on the issues covered, often accompanied by notes summarizing the leading cases. They can serve the same function as a

Restatement or legal encyclopedia in outlining a state's basic legal doctrines.

Most jurisdictions have separate publications for civil and criminal instructions. Some instructions are available on court websites, and Westlaw, Lexis, and Bloomberg Law all include instructions for federal courts and for selected states. As with many secondary sources, it may pay to check each service to determine which offers the best coverage for your needs.

CHAPTER 8

SPECIALIZED AND NONLEGAL
RESOURCES

*Images of some resources discussed in this chapter
are at* **libguides.law.virginia.edu/nutshell12/ch8**

————————

§ 8–1.   Introduction

The resources many lawyers turn to most often are
not the general treatises and case databases discussed in earlier chapters, but instead tools designed
to help them in their specific areas of law. Topical
looseleaf and electronic services make lawyers' work
easier by compiling related statutes, cases, and
regulations in one location, along with explanations,
forms, and other practice aids. These services and
other resources such as newsletters and blogs provide

the current awareness lawyers need to anticipate and respond to new legal developments, such as recently decided cases or proposed regulations.

This chapter also introduces more general sources for factual and interdisciplinary research. Reference sources can give you essential background information, and scholarship in the sciences and social sciences can expand your perspectives and insights in analyzing legal problems. They can also help you prepare for litigation or understand issues such as standard of care or trade usage.

Your first approach to finding reference information may be to run an Internet search or check Wikipedia, and in many instances this will get you just what you need. At times, however, more detailed and focused resources can still save valuable time and lead to information beyond your initial search results.

§ 8–2. Looseleaf and Electronic Services

A looseleaf service is a frequently updated resource that compiles the statutes, regulations, court decisions, administrative agency documents, and other materials in an area of law, and presents them in a cohesive manner accompanied by commentary or analysis.

The term "looseleaf" comes from the traditional manner of publication and supplementation in binders, but most modern looseleaf services are available online as well as in print. The electronic versions add the flexibility of keyword searching and the convenience of hypertext links between documents. The major looseleaf publishers all have online research platforms: Bloomberg BNA (www.bna.com), CCH IntelliConnect (intelliconnect.cch.com), RIA Checkpoint (checkpoint.riag.com), and Wolters Kluwer Cheetah (wkcheetah.com). Bloomberg Law also provides access to BNA services, and some services are also available through Westlaw or Lexis.

Looseleaf and topical reporters often contain cases that are not published elsewhere, such as trial court decisions and rulings of state and federal administrative agencies. Most services also classify and index the judicial and administrative decisions in their subject areas. These specialized digests may offer a more focused analysis of topics within their expertise than West's broader key-number digest system. BNA services are the source of Bloomberg Law's headnotes for cases in specialized areas such as employment law, environmental law, and intellectual property.

One of the most valuable features of looseleaf services is their current coverage of proposed legislation, pending litigation, and other legal developments. Many services include weekly or biweekly newsletters. With online services, you can subscribe to e-mail newsletters or set up alerts for new content that matches your keyword searches.

References in many looseleaf and online services are by *paragraph number*, a term that is used to identify a specific section of material that can vary in length from a few sentences to several pages. Each administrative decision, for example, is assigned a paragraph number for permanent reference. When using print services it is easy to be misled by the page number, but remember that this is used only for filing purposes and that the paragraph number is the point of reference used in indexes and citations.

Whether in print or online, a typical service includes several types of indexes. The general or *topical index* provides detailed subject access and is often the most effective place to begin your research, even in online services that offer full-text keyword searching. *Finding lists* provide direct references to particular statutes, regulations, or cases by their citations, and can be particularly useful in searching for numerically designated agency materials such as IRS rulings or SEC releases.

When you use a specialized looseleaf or online service for the first time, you should take a moment to familiarize yourself with its features. Guidance in print services can usually be found at the beginning of the first volume, and most online services have help sections including product tours and video explanations. A service may include features that appear confusing at first but are very useful, and a few moments of orientation can save you considerable time and frustration.

There are several ways to determine whether a service is available in an area of interest. Law review articles and cases may cite looseleaf services, and lawyers or professors specializing in a field can provide advice. The annual directory *Legal Looseleafs in Print* lists numerous print and online resources, but be aware that some are not updated very frequently. In this volume, Appendix B on pages 303–

321 covers selected looseleaf and electronic services in fields of major interest.

§ 8–3. Current Awareness

Lawyers must keep aware of developments in their areas of practice in order to give reliable advice to clients. They need to know about new court decisions, pending legislation, and agency announcements, as well as changes in the political, financial or business world. Resources to help you stay on top of the law include legal and general-interest newspapers, newsletters, and blogs.

Regular current awareness reading serves another purpose as well. Individual research assignments can build your expertise on specific questions, but they won't give you a broad understanding of an area of law. Only by reading about new developments on a regular basis will you develop the confidence that you're seeing the big picture and that your knowledge has no significant gaps. If you are new to a practice area, find out what senior attorneys are reading and sign up to see those publications.

You can create your own current awareness system using features like Westlaw's WestClip and Google Alerts (www.google.com/alerts). You set up searches on issues you want to keep track of, and the alert service automatically runs the searches daily or weekly and notifies you by e-mail when new materials match your criteria.

a. Legal Newspapers and Newsletters

News on developments in the legal profession is available from a number of daily and weekly newspapers. Legal newspapers often cover developing topics more rapidly than monthly or quarterly journals, and some also include lower court decisions that may not be reported elsewhere.

The articles and essays in legal newspapers can be hard to track down, but many newspaper websites have searchable archives available free or by subscription. One of the leading Internet sources for current legal news is law.com (www.law.com), with stories from *The National Law Journal* and regional newspapers. Other news sources include the *ABA Journal*'s Daily News (www.abajournal.com/news) and the University of Pittsburgh School of Law's JURIST (www.jurist.org). Lexis has more than a dozen legal newspapers, including *The National Law Journal* and *New York Law Journal*.

Legal newspapers across the country are listed by state in *Legal Researcher's Desk Reference* and *Legal Information Buyer's Guide & Reference Manual*. Both lists indicate frequency of publication and provide contact information and URLs.

Newsletters on specialized topics are another major source of current information in the legal world. Many newsletters have a limited circulation and can be hard to find in academic or public law libraries, but they may be the best available sources for information about newly developing areas of law. Newsletters are often the forum through which practitioners in specialized areas share information and documents. They may include copies of pleadings or other trial court documents as well as articles on recent developments. Many newsletters are available both in print and online, with e-mail notification of new developments.

Hundreds of newsletters are available through Westlaw or Lexis. Two noteworthy collections are *Westlaw Journals*, more than three dozen titles monitoring developments in areas such as bankruptcy, employment, and toxic torts; and *Mealey's Litigation Reports*, on Lexis, with more than sixty titles on topics from diet drugs to welding rods. A global search in either service will include newsletter results in Secondary Sources/Legal Newspapers and Newsletters (Westlaw) or Legal News (Lexis).

Bloomberg BNA is a major publisher of legal newsletters, in print and online through BNA.com or Bloomberg Law. Its *United States Law Week*, for example, reports every week not only on the Supreme Court, but also on new court decisions and legislative, regulatory and professional developments. Bloomberg BNA also publishes similar newsletters in dozens of specific areas that serve as major current awareness tools in their fields, including *Antitrust & Trade Regulation Report*, *Criminal Law Reporter*, *Family Law Reporter*, and *Securities Regulation & Law Report*. Many of these are supplemented by daily online updates.

Law360 (www.law360.com) is another major provider of online legal newsletters, with daily updates in more than three dozen subject areas.

Law360 claims to report on every major litigation development in the U.S. federal district courts and every major initiative by federal and state legislatures. Its stories are available to subscribers directly and through Lexis.

You can identify available newsletters for a subject area in *Legal Newsletters in Print*, which describes more than 2,200 newsletters with information about subscription prices and online access. This publication is available online, along with *Legal Looseleafs in Print*, as part of the LawTRIO database (www. infosourcespub.com).

b. Current Scholarship

Specialists need to know about scholarly as well as legal developments. A new article directly on a topic of concern may appear in any of the hundreds of law reviews and other legal journals published in this country, and may even be available online as a working paper well before publication.

Current Index to Legal Periodicals (*CILP*) (lib.law. washington.edu/cilp/cilp.html), published weekly by the University of Washington's Marian Gould Gallagher Law Library, is the leading resource on newly published law review articles. It reprints the tables of contents for more than 600 law reviews, and indexes articles under about 100 broad subject headings. Online access, limited to recent issues, is available through Westlaw.

Many scholars rely on services such as the Social Science Research Network (SSRN) (www.ssrn.com)

and the Berkeley Electronic Press (www.bepress.com) to learn of new articles and working papers. Both are major repositories for working papers and pre-publication versions of law review articles, and new work is often available here long before it appears in print. Faculty and students at subscribing institutions can also sign up for weekly e-mail notification of abstracts of new articles in any of more than a hundred LSN subject-matter e-journals.

c. Blogs and Other Online Resources

Blogs are a major vehicle for timely dissemination of news and opinion. Law blogs (sometimes called "blawgs") are written on a wide range of topics, and some have become leading sources of current information. SCOTUSblog (www.scotusblog.com), for example, often has the first report of breaking news from the Supreme Court.

You can locate blogs on particular legal topics using directories such as the *ABA Journal*'s Blawg Directory (www.abajournal.com/blawgs) and Justia BlawgSearch (blawgsearch.justia.com). Both sites link to blogs by subject, and BlawgSearch includes a feature for searching blog postings by keyword.

Other forms of social media can also be used to monitor breaking news in the legal world. Many professionals share news of legal developments through LinkedIn or Twitter. Legal Birds (legalbirds.justia.com) provides a snapshot of Twitter posts by lawyers and other legal professionals in more than fifty subject categories, and its samples may suggest specific Tweeters worth following.

E-mail listservs and discussion groups are another way to keep on top of developments in a particular area, and can also be used to seek assistance with difficult research issues. Some lists disseminate information from organizations or government agencies to subscribers, while others are designed for communities of specialists to share news and ideas. Posing questions to a list can yield replies with leads that most researchers would otherwise miss. Another subscriber may offer help with a thorny legal issue or identify a source for an obscure document. Older messages, if available in a searchable archive, are a valuable repository of information. Specialized research guides and tips from colleagues are usually the best sources of information about useful lists.

A number of courts and state legislatures offer automatic e-mail notification when a particular case or bill is acted upon, and several government agencies have mailing lists and Twitter feeds summarizing new developments. The Food and Drug Administration (www.fda.gov), for example, has dozens of update services for news on specific issues within its jurisdiction. Check agency websites for similar listservs and feeds in other fields.

§ 8–4.   Legal History Resources

Most legal research involves determining the law now in effect, but you may at times need information on legal developments occurring decades or centuries ago. The background of a court decision, statute, or constitutional provision is of more than historical interest because it can continue to influence present day interpretation.

Many of the resources discussed in earlier chapters are invaluable in legal history research. Westlaw, Lexis, and Bloomberg Law have judicial opinions back to the 18th century, and access to older law review literature is available through the comprehensive backfiles of HeinOnline (from as early as 1719) and Index to Legal Periodicals Retrospective (covering 1918–1981). Historical material from Congress is available in sources such as the digitized Serial Set publications from ProQuest and Readex, and in the Library of Congress's "A Century of Lawmaking for a New Nation: U.S. Congressional Documents and Debates, 1774–1875" (memory.loc.gov/ammem/amlaw).

In addition there are resources specifically designed for research in historical legal literature. The Making of Modern Law: Legal Treatises, 1800–1926 (gdc.gale.com) has more than 22,000 American and British works, searchable by author, title, or subject as well as full text. HeinOnline's Legal Classics Library has a more selective collection of some 6,000 titles, ranging in publication date from the 16th century through the early 21st century, that can be searched or browsed by subject.

Legal materials are also integrated within more general online book collections. Early American Imprints (www.readex.com) focuses on American works and has more than 70,000 books, pamphlets and broadsides published between 1639 and 1819. English books from the 1700s are in Eighteenth

Century Collections Online (ECCO) (gdc.gale.com), and works before 1700 can be found in Early English Books Online (EEBO) (eebo.chadwyck.com).

Other more general digitization projects such as Hathi Trust Digital Library (www.hathitrust.org), the Internet Archive's Text Archive (www.archive. org/details/texts), and Google Books (books.google. com) provide PDF access to millions of books in the public domain (generally those published before 1923) as well as searchable glimpses of more recent publications. Major works such as Sir William Blackstone's *Commentaries on the Laws of England* (1765–69) and Oliver Wendell Holmes's *The Common Law* (1881) are also available in modern facsimile printed editions, and some researchers may be able to use the original versions in rare book collections in libraries.

Other digitized resources have vastly increased access to contemporary accounts of major legal events. Reports of the drafting and ratification of the U.S. Constitution, for example, can be found in America's Historical Newspapers (www.readex.com), while the course of more modern developments such as the New Deal and civil rights litigation can be followed in ProQuest Historical Newspapers (www.proquest.com), covering several major national newspapers including the *New York Times* and *Washington Post*.

There are a variety of printed collections of historical legal documents, such as *The Documentary History of the Supreme Court of the United States, 1789–1800* (Maeva Marcus ed., 1985–2007) and

Judicial Cases Concerning American Slavery and the Negro (Helen Tunnicliff Catterall ed., 1926–37). Library online catalogs and footnote references can lead to many others.

Legal history researchers have an array of scholarly monographs from which to choose, from wide-ranging sources such as Lawrence M. Friedman, *A History of American Law* (3d ed. 2005) or *The Cambridge History of Law in America* (Michael Grossberg & Christopher Tomlins eds., 2008) to much more specific studies. One of the most significant works in American legal history is the multi-volume Oliver Wendell Holmes Devise, *History of the Supreme Court of the United States* (1971–date), which is perhaps the closest American counterpart to W. S. Holdsworth's monumental *A History of English Law* (1903–72).

Guides and bibliographies can be important resources in discovering historical materials. Works such as *Prestatehood Legal Materials: A Fifty-State Research Guide* (Michael Chiorazzi & Marguerite Most eds., 2005) have information on resources for specific jurisdictions. The predecessor to the *Index to Legal Periodicals*, entitled *Index to Legal Periodical Literature* (1888–1939), sometimes called the Jones-Chipman index after the names of its editors, covers articles as far back as 1770 and is available in HeinOnline's Law Journal Library. Morris L. Cohen, *Bibliography of Early American Law* (1998–2003) provides a comprehensive record of American legal publications up to 1860.

§ 8–5.   Statistics

Lawyers need demographic and statistical information for many purposes, from preparing for cross-examination of an expert witness to supporting a discrimination claim. Some statistical sources focus on legal matters, while others are more general.

Statistics on the federal courts, such as the number of cases commenced and terminated by district and by subject, can be found in the Administrative Office of the U.S. Courts' annual *Judicial Business of the United States Courts* and on its website (www.uscourts.gov). The National Center for State Courts site has a Court Statistics Project (www. courtstatistics.org) that offers several ways to query its statistical database and examine state court business. It includes the annual publication *Examining the Work of State Courts*, as well as caseload statistics and court structure charts.

Criminal statistics are available from both federal and state governments. The Federal Bureau of Investigation issues *Uniform Crime Reports* (also known as Crime in the United States) in print and online (www.fbi.gov/about-us/cjis/ucr), focusing on criminal activities. Sourcebook of Criminal Justice Statistics (www.albany.edu/sourcebook/) has a broader survey of the social and economic impacts of crime. The Bureau of Justice Statistics website (www.bjs.gov) has links to a variety of other statistics and publications.

The American Bar Foundation's *Lawyer Statistical Report* is the leading source on the composition of the

U.S. legal profession. The most recent report, published in 2012, has data as of 2005. The American Bar Association's Legal Profession Statistics page (www.americanbar.org/resources_for_lawyers/ profession_statistics/) has links to various websites with information on the legal profession, including demographics and salaries.

The U.S. Census Bureau (www.census.gov) prepares the Census of Population and Housing every ten years, and all censuses since 1790 are available on its website (www.census.gov/prod/www/ decennial.html). The Bureau also undertakes an Economic Census on business and industry every five years (www.census.gov/econ/). To find economic information about a particular industry, you will usually need to determine its North American Industry Classification System (NAICS) code (www. census.gov/eos/www/naics/). The NAICS page also has information on the older Standard Industrial Classification (SIC) system which it replaced, but which is still used by some sources.

The *Statistical Abstract of the United States* was published annually through 2012 by the Census Bureau in print and online, and has been continued beginning in 2013 by ProQuest (statabs.proquest. com/sa/). This basic reference source covers a wide range of economic and demographic statistics, and is particularly useful because it gives source information for each table. It thus serves as a convenient lead to agencies and publications with more thorough coverage of specific areas.

The government's *Statistical Abstract* website has previous editions of the publication, all the way back to 1878. *Historical Statistics of the United States: Earliest Times to the Present* (Susan B. Carter et al. eds., 2006), available in a five-volume printed set and online (hsus.cambridge.org), is a comprehensive compendium of statistics from the *Statistical Abstract* and hundreds of other sources. Another source for statistics from government agencies is the FedStats website (fedstats.sites.usa.gov), with links to numerous federal statistical sources by topic and by agency. You can also download free "raw" datasets from government agencies at Data.gov (www.data.gov).

Annual reports and other publications of government agencies, trade associations, labor unions, and public interest groups generally contain statistical data relating to their work and interests. ProQuest Statistical Insight (statistical.proquest.com) provides access to much of this material, adding more than 100,000 tables each year.

Most statistical sources focus on facts rather than opinions, but surveys can be important resources in many areas of the law from employment discrimination to trademark infringement. Polls and other sources of public opinion are available through a number of electronic sources. Gallup, Inc. (www.gallup.com) has recent poll results and allows keyword searching of questionnaires and poll analyses on major topics. The subscription resources Polling the Nations (poll.orspub.com) and the Roper Center for Public Opinion Research (www.ropercenter.edu)

have survey data from hundreds of organizations, accessible by keyword search or through subject indexes.

§ 8–6.   Legal Directories

Chapters 5 through 7 discussed directories covering federal and state governments, including legislatures, administrative agencies, and courts. Directories of lawyers and legal organizations have background information about other lawyers and can help you establish contacts within the profession. Organizations interested in particular issues may be able to provide you with insights not available in any printed or electronic sources.

Numerous directories have contact and biographical information for lawyers. Most focus on individual states or particular specialties, but two comprehensive directories of the legal profession are published by divisions of the parent companies of Westlaw and Lexis. Each covers close to a million lawyers, but neither includes every lawyer in the country.

The *Martindale-Hubbell Law Directory* is the more established source, dating to the nineteenth century. Its online version (www.martindale.com) is the most inclusive. Free listings have only mailing addresses and basic information about education and bar admission dates, but in some instances these are accompanied by ratings and comments from fellow attorneys and clients. Attorneys and law firms can purchase fuller entries with telephone numbers, e-mail addresses, and more extensive biographical information, and website links. Martindale-Hubbell's listings are also available on Lexis as the LexisNexis Law Directory, without peer or client evaluations, and in an annual printed edition of four volumes limited to lawyers and law firms that have purchased listings.

West Legal Directory (WLD), the other nationwide directory of attorneys, is available on Westlaw. For most attorneys listed, in addition to addresses and telephone numbers it has biographical information such as education, professional affiliations, and areas of practice. Entries include tabs linking to relevant cases, briefs, pleadings, and other documents, and to a Litigation History Report summarizing the types of cases an attorney has handled. The FindLaw Lawyer Directory (lawyers.findlaw.com) is a free version of the directory with basic contact information.

Several other national directories of lawyers and law firms are available, although none is as comprehensive as *Martindale-Hubbell* or WLD. *Who's Who in American Law* has biographical information on prominent attorneys and legal scholars, and *The Best Lawyers in America* (www.bestlawyers.com) is a guide to highly respected practicing attorneys, listed by state and city under about seventy specialties. Two sources for information on the management and recruiting personnel of major law firms are *Law Firms Yellow Book* (www.leadershipdirectories.com) and the National Association for Law Placement's *Directory of Legal Employers* (www.nalpdirectory. com).

Other directories focus on attorneys working outside of law firms. *Directory of Corporate Counsel* (available on Westlaw) has biographical information on lawyers working for companies and nonprofit organizations. Directories of public interest lawyers include *Directory of Legal Aid and Defender Offices in the United States.*

State and regional directories often have more thorough listings of local lawyers than national directories. Legal Directories Publishing Co. publishes directories for about twenty states and offers a free online lawyer search (www.legaldirectories.com). Many state and local bar associations also publish directories or offer attorney search features on their websites. The ABA has links to these sites (www.americanbar.org/groups/bar_services/).

Professional and trade organizations can provide a wealth of information in their areas of interest. Two directories are notable for their broad coverage of both legal and nonlegal organizations. *Encyclopedia of Associations* (available online as Associations Unlimited (www.cengage.com)) has descriptions and contact information for more than 25,000 national organizations. *National Trade and Professional Associations of the United States* (www.associationexecs.com) is less broad in scope but just as useful for basic information on major business-related organizations.

§ 8–7. General News and Business Information

Legal newspapers focus on law-related activity, but for a broader picture of developments in business, politics and society it is necessary to monitor more general sources such as newspapers or news websites. In addition to their value for current awareness, news stories can also be rich sources for factual research or background information.

Westlaw, Lexis and Bloomberg Law are among the most convenient news sources for law students. Each has hundreds of newspapers, wire services, and business publications. The services have considerable overlap in coverage, but each has sources not found in the others; only Lexis, for example, has the full text of the *Wall Street Journal*.

Other online sources of news include websites for individual newspapers and multisource subscription services such as Factiva (www.factiva.com). Google News (news.google.com) has free, current coverage of a wide range of newspapers, magazines, and wire services.

Business developments are a major focus of research in news sources. Information on companies can often be found through their websites, but a number of print and online business directories are published. The amount of available information on a company depends in part on whether it is publicly or privately held. Because public companies must report to their shareholders and government regulators, they publish far more information. Basic data on public corporations is available in sources such as Hoover's Company Records and LexisNexis Corporate Affiliations, both available on Lexis.

Ward's Business Directory of U.S. Private and Public Companies (www.cengage.com) includes information on more than 100,000 privately held companies. The broadest databases, such as Dun & Bradstreet Business Directory (www.dandb.com/businessdirectory) and Mergent Online (www.mergentonline.com) cover millions of public and private businesses and have basic contact information and employment data.

Business entities generate voluminous public record filings. Publicly held corporations must file a number of documents with the Securities and Exchange Commission, including annual and quarterly financial reports, and these are available free through the SEC's EDGAR system (www.sec.gov/edgar.shtml). SEC filings are also accessible through several subscription services, including Westlaw, Lexis, and Bloomberg Law. Both public and private companies must register with secretaries of state or similar state offices. Secretary of State Corporate and Business Entity Search (www.secstates.com) has links to searchable corporation registries in each state, most of which provide basic information such as addresses, officers, and registered agents.

§ 8–8.   Interdisciplinary Research

In either law school or legal practice, the use of secondary sources for background information and analysis is rarely limited to treatises and law review articles. Work from other disciplines can explain the policy bases for legal rules or add insights to buttress legal arguments. Practicing lawyers need nonlegal literature for several purposes, from investigating issues such as the standard of care to preparing for expert witness depositions.

General Periodical Databases and Indexes.
Indexes to nonlegal periodical literature can supply
valuable leads that might never be found through
law reviews. Some of these are specialized indexes in
particular disciplines, while others have comprehensive coverage of a wide range of sources (sometimes
including legal journals). The online versions of many
indexes link directly to the full text of articles listed.

Indexes from other disciplines such as
ABI/INFORM (business and economics), America:
History & Life (U.S. and Canadian history), EconLit
(economics), PsycINFO (psychology and related
disciplines), or Sociological Abstracts may offer background information or interdisciplinary perspectives.
Most of these databases include searchable abstracts,
which can be invaluable both in finding articles and
in identifying whether they would be of value.

Web of Science (www.webofknowledge.com) is a
very broad index covering more than 12,000 journals.
You can search for articles by author or title keyword,
and you can run a "Cited Reference Search" to find
articles citing a particular author or source.

Other major multidisciplinary indexes, one or
more of which may be available by subscription at an
academic library, include EBSCOhost Academic
Search Complete (www.ebscohost.com), InfoTrac
OneFile (www.cengage.com), and ProQuest Central
(www.proquest.com). All of these databases serve as
one-stop shops for a wide range of journal literature.

IngentaConnect (www.ingentaconnect.com) also
has comprehensive coverage of current journal

literature, with tables of contents information from more than 10,000 publications. One advantage of IngentaConnect is that searching is free to researchers unaffiliated with subscribing institutions. Most articles are available for fee-based download by nonsubscribers.

JSTOR (www.jstor.org) provides retrospective coverage of more than 2,000 scholarly journals in a wide range of disciplines, including several dozen major law reviews and legal journals. Articles can be found through keyword searches and downloaded in PDF. Another subscription web service with the full text of journal articles from as far back as 1802 is Periodicals Archive Online (www.proquest.com).

Dissertations. Doctoral dissertations are valuable sources of scholarly research that are often overlooked by law students and lawyers. A dissertation is the product of several years of research, and it usually includes an introductory survey of the literature and an exhaustive bibliography of published and manuscript sources. These documents were once esoteric and hard-to-find, but digital access now makes them readily available as research tools. ProQuest Dissertations & Theses Global (www.proquest.com) has most dissertations since 1997 as well as selected earlier works. (It also indexes older dissertations back to 1861.)

Online Catalogs. No law library has every possible text, and interlibrary loan is an invaluable resource for lawyers and scholars. WorldCat (www.worldcat.org) is a free resource with records for more than two billion items, in thousands of libraries worldwide. An Advanced Search screen allows you to combine keywords with words in the Author, Title or Subject fields and to limit results by date. Once a relevant text is found, its record lists libraries in which it is found and usually provides links to individual libraries' online catalogs.

You can also search specific library catalogs, including the Library of Congress (catalog.loc.gov). Several websites, including Wikipedia, have lists of links to law school websites, from which other library catalogs can be reached.

Other Reference Sources. Most disciplines have various encyclopedias, dictionaries, research guides, directories, indexes, and other sources that may help you with a research project if you know where to look. One way to discover available resources is through the American Library Association's Guide to Reference (www.guidetoreference.org), which covers hundreds of disciplines. It is available free but will not be updated after January 2016.

§ 8–9. Specialized Research Guides

This Nutshell examines legal research generally, but researchers should be aware that specialized areas of law have many idiosyncrasies. Specialized research guides have been published as monographs and in journals such as *Law Library Journal* and *Legal Reference Services Quarterly*. Many law libraries have research guides to specialized areas on their websites, so a first approach may be to run a general search such as "environmental law research guide." More than 430,000 publicly available research guides across the library community can be searched at the LibGuides Community website (libguides.com).

Specialized Legal Research (Penny A. Hazelton ed., 2014 ed.) covers more than a dozen topics, with chapters on admiralty, banking law, copyright, customs, environmental law, government contracts, immigration, income tax, labor and employment law, military and veterans law, patents and trademarks, securities regulation, and the Uniform Commercial Code. The volume also includes a bibliography of other specialized legal research sources. Tax research is the focus of several published works, including Joni Larson & Dan Sheaffer, *Federal Tax Research* (2d ed. 2011) and Gail Levin Richmond, *Federal Tax Research: Guide to Materials and Techniques* (9th ed. 2014).

Legal materials can vary greatly from state to state, and law library websites often have guidance on legal research issues in their home jurisdictions. Appendix A on pages 291–302 lists state-specific research guides, which can provide valuable details and information on sources.

CHAPTER 9

INTERNATIONAL LAW

Images of some resources discussed in this chapter are at **libguides.law.virginia.edu/nutshell12/ch9**

---

§ 9–1.   Introduction

Public international law is the body of rules and procedures governing relations among nations. Although its primary historical functions have been the preservation of peace and regulation of war, international law now governs an ever broader range of transnational activities. It regulates matters from copyright protection to the rights of refugees, and agreements such as the Convention on Contracts for the International Sale of Goods (CISG) have made international law an inherent aspect of commercial activity. *Public international law* is distinguished from *private international law* (or conflict of laws), which determines where, and by whose law, controversies involving more than one jurisdiction are resolved, as well as how foreign judgments are enforced.

A modern legal practice often requires knowledge of international and foreign law. If you are representing an American firm investing in another country, for example, you must be aware of treaties between the two nations as well as the investment and trade laws of both the United States and the other country. You may also need to examine jurisdictional issues in resolving disputes or in determining the application of one country's rules in the other's courts. This chapter focuses on international law, while research in the law of foreign countries is the subject of Chapter 10.

The classic statement of the sources of international law is Article 38 of the Statute of the International Court of Justice, identifying the bases on which it decides disputes:

(a) international conventions, whether general or particular, establishing rules expressly recognized by the contesting States;

(b) international custom, as evidence of a general practice accepted as law;

(c) the general principles of law recognized by civilized nations;

(d) . . . judicial decisions and the teachings of the most highly qualified publicists [scholars] of the various nations, as subsidiary means for the determination of rules of law.

International conventions (treaties) and *international custom* are generally considered the two most important sources. If a treaty is relevant to a problem involving its signatories, it is the primary legal authority. International custom is the actual conduct of nations, provided it is consistent with the rule of law. Custom is not defined in specific legal sources but is established by evidence of state practices. *General principles of law* are the most amorphous of the sources but are usually considered to be basic principles articulated in the classic texts of international law. *Judicial decisions* and *scholarly writings* are less important than treaties and international custom. Cases are generally not considered binding precedents in subsequent disputes, but they can aid in interpreting treaties and in defining custom.

§ 9–2. Preliminary Research

As in other areas, the first step in approaching most research problems in international law is to turn to a reference work, a treatise, or a law review article for general information and for help in analyzing the issues involved.

Encyclopedias and Treatises. The leading reference work in international law, *Max Planck Encyclopedia of Public International Law* (Rüdiger Wolfrum ed., 2012) (opil.ouplaw.com/home/EPIL), is a ten-volume work providing a comprehensive view of international law issues. Its articles are written by respected authorities and include brief bibliographies for further research.

Edmund Jan Osmańczyk, *Encyclopedia of the United Nations and International Agreements* (Anthony Mango ed., 3d ed. 2003) is another multivolume encyclopedia with wide coverage of international law issues, as well as excerpts from treaties and other major documents. Shorter reference works include Anthony Aust, *Handbook of International Law* (2d ed. 2010) and *Routledge Handbook of International Law* (David Armstrong ed., 2009).

Several general treatises provide overviews of international law doctrine. *Oppenheim's International Law* (Robert Jennings & Arthur Watts eds., 9th ed. 1992) is considered a classic work. More modern treatises include James Crawford, *Brownlie's Principles of Public International Law* (8th ed. 2012) and Malcolm N. Shaw, *International Law* (7th ed. 2014). *The Oxford Guide to Treaties* (Duncan B. Hollis ed., 2012) explains issues of treaty formation and interpretation. The American Law Institute's *Restatement of the Law, Third, Foreign Relations Law of the United States* (1987) summarizes American law and practice in international law and foreign relations. The Institute is currently in the process of preparing a *Restatement, Fourth* on the topic, and drafts are available on HeinOnline.

Journal Articles. International law has numerous scholarly periodicals, including more than seventy specialized journals published at U.S. law schools. Among the more prestigious professional journals are the *American Journal of International Law* and *International and Comparative Law Quarterly.* Many national societies of international law produce annual publications such as the *British Yearbook of International Law* or the *Annuaire Français de Droit International*, most of which contain scholarly articles as well as reprints of selected major documents. Many of these yearbooks and other sources are available in HeinOnline's Foreign and International Law Resources Database.

International law topics are well represented in the standard law review literature, and articles can be found through any of the full-text and index resources discussed in Chapter 2. *Index to Foreign Legal Periodicals* (1960–date, available through HeinOnline) principally covers journals published in countries outside the common law system, but it also indexes articles on international law in selected American law reviews. *Public International Law: A Current Bibliography of Books and Articles* (1975–date) is a comprehensive index of the literature in the field.

Dictionaries. International law has its own specialized terminology, and a dictionary can help you understand key concepts. The leading work is

Parry & Grant Encyclopaedic Dictionary of International Law (John P. Grant & J. Craig Barker eds., 3d ed. 2009), which has descriptive entries with citations to major sources. James R. Fox, *Dictionary of International and Comparative Law* (3d ed. 2003) has more concise definitions of terms.

§ 9–3.   U.S. Practice in International Law

For American lawyers and law students, materials on United States practice are the most frequently consulted research sources in international law. These include treaties and the materials needed to interpret them, as well as documents dealing with issues in U.S. foreign relations.

a. Treaties

Treaties are formal agreements between countries, and they have legal significance for both domestic and international purposes. Article VI of the U.S. Constitution provides that treaties are part of the supreme law of the land, giving them the same legal effect and status as federal statutes. Treaties and statutes can supersede each other as the controlling law within the United States, but a treaty that is no longer valid as U.S. law may still be binding in international law.

Treaty research generally involves several aspects: (1) finding its text in an authoritative source; (2) determining whether it is in force and with what parties and reservations; and (3) interpreting its provisions, with the aid of commentaries, judicial decisions, and legislative history. What resources to use depends in part on whether the United States is a party to a treaty or convention.

Anthony Aust, *Modern Treaty Law and Practice* (3d ed. 2013) and *National Treaty Law and Practice* (Duncan B. Hollis et al. eds., 2005) both analyze treaty interpretation and practice, in the United States and generally.

Treaty Process. Treaties between two governments are called *bilateral*, and those entered into by more than two governments are called *multilateral*. Parties' initial signatures to a treaty establish their agreement that its text is authentic and definitive, but nations are not bound until they approve the treaty through ratification (such as approval by two-thirds of the U.S. Senate) or some other procedure. Parties to multilateral treaties may add what are known as RUDs: *Reservations* excluding certain provisions, and *Understandings* or *Declarations* providing their own interpretations of treaty terms. The text of a treaty usually identifies the event that triggers its entry into force, often (in the case of multilateral conventions) when a specified number of nations have indicated their approval.

The President makes *executive agreements* with other countries under the Article II authority to conduct foreign affairs. These are similar in effect to treaties, but they do not require Senate approval and hence are often used to streamline the process and avoid controversy. The sources and research procedures discussed in this section generally apply to both treaties and executive agreements.

Sources. Treaties before 1950 were published in the *Statutes at Large* and have been reprinted in *Treaties and Other International Agreements of the United States of America 1776–1949* (Charles I. Bevans comp., 1968–75, available on HeinOnline). Beginning in 1950, *United States Treaties and Other International Agreements* (*UST*) became the official, permanent form of publication for treaties and executive agreements to which the United States is a party.

UST, however, was only published through volume 35 (1983–84). The only official source for more recent treaties is a numbered series of separately paginated documents, *Treaties and Other International Acts Series* (*TIAS*), now available on the Department of State website (www.state.gov/s/l/treaty/). *TIAS* was issued in pamphlet form through 2006, but is now published only online.

Commercial services are important sources for current treaties and retrospective coverage. Westlaw and Lexis have comprehensive treaty coverage from the 1770s through recent months. HeinOnline has a U.S. Treaties and Agreements Library with PDF versions of treaties in *Statutes at Large*, *UST*, and *TIAS*, as well as recent treaties not yet published in these sources.

A citation to a treaty includes its name, the date of its signing, the parties (if there are only two or three), and references to the main sources of publication. The signing date is particularly important because it is used to identify treaties in most lists and indexes. *The Bluebook* generally specifies citation of bilateral treaties to an official U.S. source, if available; for multilateral treaties, a parallel citation to an official international source, usually the *United Nations Treaty Series* (*UNTS*), may be added.

Guides and Indexes. Treaties are generally published chronologically rather than by subject, so you many need a guide or index to identify agreements with a specific country or on a particular topic and to determine the status of a treaty.

Treaties in Force (www.state.gov/s/l/treaty/), an annual publication of the Department of State, is the official index to current United States treaties and agreements. It has citations to all of the major treaty publications, including *Stat.*, *UST*, *TIAS*, and *UNTS*. The first section of *Treaties in Force* lists bilateral treaties by country and, under each country, by subject; and the second section lists multilateral treaties by subject. Westlaw and Lexis have the current *Treaties in Force*, and HeinOnline has current and past editions back to 1929.

Kavass's Guide to the United States Treaties in Force, issued annually in print and on HeinOnline, has subject and country indexes to both bilateral and multilateral treaties. These can be useful because the official *Treaties in Force* doesn't index bilateral treaties by subject or list multilateral conventions by country.

The major collections of U.S. treaties are indexed by subject, date, and country in *United States Treaty Index Consolidation* (Igor I. Kavass ed., 2001–date), which is updated semiannually by *Kavass' Current Treaty Index*, available in print and on HeinOnline.

Sometimes one of the hardest steps in researching a treaty is identifying its *UST* and *UNTS* citations. Lists such as the University of Minnesota Law School's "Frequently-Cited Treaties and Other International Instruments" (libguides.law.umn.edu/frequentlycitedtreaties) can help. Searching an online law review database for the title or subject of a treaty will often lead to numerous footnotes providing the necessary references.

Interpretation. Like statutes or constitutional provisions, most treaties contain ambiguities that can lead to controversies in interpretation and application. Several resources assist in understanding treaty terms, including court decisions and documents produced during a treaty's drafting and consideration. You can learn of cases from law review articles and other secondary sources, or by using a treaty's name or citation in a full-text case law search.

The *United States Code Service* includes two volumes that can serve as starting points for finding cases. "International Agreements" contains the texts of about three dozen major conventions and treaties, accompanied by research references and case annotations, and "Annotations to Uncodified Laws and Treaties" has broader coverage of decisions interpreting other U.S. treaties. Lexis includes the first volume, under the title USCS—International Conventions.

Records of Senate ratification can illuminate the terms and meaning of U.S. treaties. *Treaty Documents* (until 1980, called *Senate Executive Documents*) contain treaties transmitted to the Senate for its consideration, and usually include messages from the President and the Secretary of State. The Senate Foreign Relations Committee analyzes treaties and issues *Senate Executive Reports* with its recommendations. Both Treaty Documents and Senate Executive Reports are issued in numbered series identifying the Congress and sequence in which they were issued. ProQuest Congressional includes coverage of Senate treaty materials back to 1817.

Congress.gov has legislative history summaries of treaty action since the 90th Congress (1967–68), with links to Treaty Documents. The looseleaf *Congressional Index* also includes a table of treaties pending before the Senate, with references to documents, reports, hearings, and ratifications.

b. Foreign Relations Documents

State practice is the primary evidence of custom, one of the major sources of international law. To study state practice, you will need to turn to sources that explain how a particular nation has acted in the past.

Reference works such as *Encyclopedia of U.S. Foreign Relations* (Bruce W. Jentleson & Thomas G. Paterson eds., 1997) can provide a background for understanding U.S. practice. You will find more detailed discussion in a series prepared by the Department of State, *Digest of United States Practice in International Law*. This set compiles excerpts from treaties, decisions, diplomatic correspondence, and other documents reflecting the U.S. position on major issues of international law, accompanied by explanatory commentary. The Department of State website (www.state.gov/s/l/c8183.htm) has digests since 1989, with links to the full text of documents excerpted in those volumes.

The Department of State also published earlier encyclopedic digests of U.S. practice that may be of value for historical research. These digests, commonly known by the names of their compilers (Wharton, Moore, Hackworth, and Whiteman), are all available in HeinOnline's Foreign and International Law Resources Database.

Much more documentation of U.S. practice is in *Foreign Relations of the United States* (1861–date), a comprehensive record of material relating to such issues as treaty negotiation and international conflicts. There is a time lag of more than thirty years between the original (often confidential) issuance of documents and their publication in this series. The set from 1861 to 1960 is available online from the University of Wisconsin (uwdc.library.wisc.edu/collections/FRUS), and selected volumes from 1945 to 1980 are available from the Department of State website (history.state.gov).

§ 9–4.   General Treaty Research

The United States is not a party to every major multilateral treaty. The United Nations Convention on the Law of the Sea and the Vienna Convention on the Law of Treaties are just two of the many agreements that the U.S. has not ratified. Regional agreements in other parts of the world and bilateral treaties between other countries may also be important in your research. In addition to the U.S. treaty resources already discussed, more general resources are frequently needed as well.

Sources. The standard official source for modern treaties is the *United Nations Treaty Series* (*UNTS*), containing more than 2,400 volumes and available free online as the United Nations Treaty Collection (treaties.un.org). Since 1946 this series has published all treaties registered with the UN by member nations in their original languages, as well as in English and French translations.

The United Nations Treaty Collection website includes summaries and information on ratification status as well as treaty texts. Its "Overview" section has reference material explaining the treaty process and defining terminology. Search options include popular name, title, and full text, but there isn't a simple way to find documents by volume and page number.

UNTS treaties are also available as part of HeinOnline's World Treaty Library. This comprehensive online collection of treaties covers more than 180,000 agreements back to 1648, including every major U.S. and international treaty series. HeinOnline is often a more convenient source than the UN site, particularly if you want to retrieve treaties by citation.

Treaties predating the creation of the United Nations can be found in two older series. The *League of Nations Treaty Series* (*LNTS*) (1920–46) is similar in scope to the *UNTS*, and is included in the online United Nations Treaty Collection. A retrospective collection, *Consolidated Treaty Series* (*CTS*), contains all treaties between nation states from 1648 to 1919. Both *LNTS* and *CTS* are available from HeinOnline, and *CTS* is also online as *Oxford Historical Treaties* (opil.ouplaw.com/home/oht).

Regional organizations also publish compilations of treaties among their members. The African Union (au.int/en/treaties), Council of Europe (conventions.coe.int), and Organization of American States (www.oas.org/DIL/) all have online collections of major treaties. The Hague Conference on Private International Law (www.hcch.net) has the text of several dozen conventions it has drafted on issues such as international civil procedure and recognition of judgments. Many countries publish current treaties in their official gazettes and on government websites, and new treaties are often printed in international law yearbooks and journals.

The American Society of International Law's Electronic Information System for International Law (EISIL) (www.eisil.org) has thousands of links to treaties and other documents in fourteen major subject areas. In addition to links to the primary sources, each record also includes a "More Information" button with citations, dates, and brief descriptions.

Indexes and Status Tables. The leading online index to multilateral conventions is the Flare Index to Treaties (ials.sas.ac.uk/treatyindex.htm). It has basic information such as official titles and dates for more than 2,000 multilateral treaties, as well as citations to printed versions and links to online sources for the treaty text.

Multilateral Treaties Deposited with the Secretary-General (MTDSG), available online from the United Nations (treaties.un.org), is a leading source for determining the status of and identifying the parties to major conventions. This listing of several hundred treaties is arranged by subject, and provides citations, information on status, a list of parties with dates of signature and ratification, and the text of any reservations imposed by individual parties. Coverage in MTDSG is limited to treaties concluded under UN auspices or for which the Secretary-General acts as depository, so it excludes some major agreements such as CITES (www.cites.org) and the Geneva Conventions of 1949 (www.icrc.org/ihl). These organizations' sites have status information, as well as treaty texts and other documents. Even conventions covered by MTDSG may have websites with much more detailed information.

The *United Nations Treaty Series* has indexes for every 50 or 100 volumes, but no cumulative official index. This is less significant now that the United Nations Treaty Collection is available free online, but retrospective access by subject and country back to 1946 is provided by a commercial publication, *United*

Nations Cumulative Treaty Index (1999), and through HeinOnline.

Interpretation. Scholarly commentary and judicial decisions are the standard sources of treaty interpretation. Additional resources available for some multilateral conventions are the *travaux preparatoires* (documents created during the drafting process such as reports and debates). These are recognized under the 1969 Vienna Convention on the Law of Treaties as a source for clarifying ambiguous treaty terms. *Travaux* can be difficult to find, but they have been compiled and published for several conventions. The Yale Law Library has a guide to *travaux* collections (library.law.yale.edu/foreign/collected-travaux), with links to online sources and tables of contents of published works.

§ 9–5. Cases and Arbitrations

Although most disputes between nations are resolved by direct negotiation, some are submitted to international tribunals, arbitral bodies, or specially convened commissions. Courts established by regional organizations resolve cases between nations and their citizens, and are developing a growing body of international human rights law. Decisions of domestic courts on matters of international law can also be important sources, particularly as evidence of international legal custom.

a. International Court of Justice

The preeminent international tribunal is the International Court of Justice (ICJ), also known as the World Court, which settles legal disputes between nations. The ICJ was created in 1945 by the Charter of the United Nations, succeeding the Permanent Court of International Justice (PCIJ) of the League of Nations. The Court meets at The Hague and consists of fifteen justices elected to nine-year terms.

The ICJ issues only a handful of decisions each year. These are published in *Reports of Judgments, Advisory Opinions and Orders* and are available on the ICJ website (www.icj-cij.org). The site has material from every case the Court has heard since its inception and from cases heard by the PCIJ, as well as information on the current docket and basic documents such as the Statute of the Court and rules.

Decisions are also available through online services such as Westlaw and HeinOnline's United Nations Law Collection. *International Law Reports* (1956–date) and its predecessor *Annual Digest and Reports of Public International Law Cases* (1932–55) contain all PCIJ and ICJ decisions, as well as English translations of selected decisions of regional and national courts on international law issues. Leading commentaries on the ICJ include Robert Kolb, *The Elgar Companion to the International Court of Justice* (2014); Shabtai Rosenne, *The Law and Practice of the International Court, 1920–2005* (4th ed. 2006); and *The Statute of the International Court of Justice: A Commentary* (Andreas Zimmermann et al. eds., 2d ed. 2012).

b. Other Courts

The ICJ is not the only court of international scope. Various conventions and organizations have established courts to adjudicate disputes among nations or to deal with specific issues such as genocide, human rights, or the law of the sea. The Project on International Courts and Tribunals (www.pict-pcti.org) has information on dozens of global and regional tribunals, with links to cases and basic documents.

Summaries of courts' organizations and procedures can be found in *Manual on International Courts and Tribunals* (Ruth Mackenzie et al. eds., 2d ed. 2010), and *The Rules, Practice, and Jurisprudence of International Courts and Tribunals* (Chiara Giorgetti ed., 2012). The World Legal Information Institute's International Courts & Tribunals Collection (www.worldlii.org/int/cases/) allows searching across thousands of decisions from more than thirty of these courts.

International Courts. An International Criminal Court (www.icc-cpi.int) with jurisdiction over war crimes, genocide, and crimes against humanity had its first session in 2003. Its jurisdiction has been accepted by more than 120 countries, but not by the United States. Cases, documents, and background information are available on the court's website, and *The Annotated Digest of the International Criminal Court* has abstracts of its developing case law. Major secondary sources include William Schabas, *The International Criminal Court: A Commentary on the Rome Statute* (2010).

More specialized courts address violations of international humanitarian law in specific countries. These include the International Criminal Tribunal for the former Yugoslavia (ICTY) (www.icty.org), the International Criminal Tribunal for Rwanda (ICTR) (www.unictr.org), and Extraordinary Chambers in the Courts of Cambodia (www.eccc.gov.kh). Documents and judgments are available on the court websites, and major cases can be found in *Annotated Leading Cases of International Criminal Tribunals* (www.annotatedleadingcases.com). Reference works in the area include *The Oxford Companion to International Criminal Justice* (Antonio Cassese ed., 2009) and *Routledge Handbook of International Criminal Law* (William Schabas & Nadia Bernaz eds., 2011).

Another court of worldwide scope, the International Tribunal for the Law of the Sea (ITLOS) (www.itlos.org), was created by the United Nations Convention on the Law of the Sea and established in 1996. More than 160 countries (not including the United States) are parties to the convention. ITLOS rules and cases are available on its website, and publications include P. Chandrasekhara Rao & Ph. Gautier, *The Rules of the International Tribunal for the Law of the Sea: A Commentary* (2006).

Regional Courts. The decisions of the courts of regional organizations have assumed growing importance in international law as the range of disputes over which they exercise jurisdiction grows.

The European Court of Justice (curia.europa.eu), an organ of the European Union, resolves disputes between EU institutions and member states over the interpretation and application of EU treaties and legislation. A subordinate General Court (formerly the Court of First Instance) handles the initial hearing in most cases. All decisions since the Court of Justice's inception are available on its website, as well as through Westlaw and other online services. Print sources include the official *Reports of Cases*, *Common Market Law Reports*, and *European Union Law Reporter*. Commentaries include Bertrand Wägenbaur, *Court of Justice of the EU: Commentary on Statute and Rules of Procedure* (2013).

The European Court of Human Rights (www.echr.coe.int) was created under the European Convention of Human Rights of 1950 for the international protection of the rights of individuals. The Court's website has basic texts and searchable case law. Decisions are published officially in *Reports of Judgments and Decisions*, and are also reported commercially in *European Human Rights Reports* (available in Westlaw). A variety of documents and decisions appear in the annual *Yearbook of the European Convention on Human Rights*. Secondary sources include William Schabas, *The European Convention on Human Rights: A Commentary* (2015).

The Inter-American Commission on Human Rights (www.oas.org/en/iachr/) hears complaints of individuals and institutions alleging violations of human rights in the American countries. The Commission, or a member state, can refer matters to the Inter-American Court of Human Rights (www. corteidh.or.cr). Twenty-five countries (not including the United States) have accepted its jurisdiction. The Court's decisions are reported in print and on its website. The *Inter-American Yearbook on Human Rights* covers the work of both the Commission and the Court and includes selected decisions and other documents. The IACHR Project at Loyola Law School, Los Angeles (iachr.lls.edu) has a database of Court decisions that can be searched by case name, country, topic, or specific treaty violation, and commentaries include Laurence Burgorgue-Larsen & Amaya Úbeda de Torres, *The Inter-American Court of Human Rights: Case-Law and Commentary* (2011).

The African Court on Human and Peoples' Rights (en.african-court.org) delivered its first judgment in 2009. Its website has basic documents and information on its cases. The African Human Rights Case Law Analyser (caselaw.ihrda.org) covers both the African Court and regional tribunals. For background, see works such as Frans Viljoen, *International Human Rights Law in Africa* (2d ed. 2012).

National Courts. Cases from domestic courts often address issues of international law, and their decisions can have both domestic and international significance. As mentioned earlier, *International Law Reports* contains decisions of national courts on international law issues. The International Crimes Database (ICD) (www.internationalcrimesdatabase. org) has documents from both international and domestic courts. The new *ALR International* series, available on Westlaw, summarizes U.S. and foreign cases on issues such as the construction and application of specific articles of major multilateral conventions.

Cases from the U.S. and other countries under the Convention on Contracts for the International Sale of Goods (CISG) are available through UNILEX (www.unilex.info) and Pace University's Institute of International Commercial Law (www.cisg.law.pace.edu). Case Law on UNCITRAL Texts (CLOUT) (www.uncitral.org/uncitral/en/case_law.html) has international trade law cases, and ECOLEX (www.ecolex.org) is a gateway to environmental law decisions by national and international courts as well as treaties, legislation and other resources.

c. Arbitrations

Many disputes, both between nations and between commercial partners, are settled by arbitration. Arbitrations between nations are published in the United Nations series, *Reports of International Arbitral Awards* (*RIAA*), available online from the UN (www.un.org/law/riaa/) and from HeinOnline. Older arbitral decisions back to 1794 are reprinted in *Repertory of International Arbitral Jurisprudence* (1989–91).

Several sources cover international arbitrations between private parties, including *Mealey's International Arbitration Report* (available in Lexis), *World Arbitration Reporter*, and *Yearbook: Commercial Arbitration*. Recent treatises in the area include Margaret L. Moses, *The Principles and Practice of International Commercial Arbitration* (2d ed. 2012) and *Practitioner's Handbook on International Commercial Arbitration* (Frank-Bernd Weigand ed., 2d ed. 2009). Kluwer Arbitration (www.kluwerarbitration.com) has access to a variety of major sources, including conventions, rules, and case law.

§ 9–6.   International Organizations

National governments are the major parties in international law, but worldwide and regional intergovernmental organizations (IGOs) play a vital role by establishing norms, promoting multilateral conventions, and providing mechanisms for the peaceful resolution of conflicts. Even when not acting as lawmaking bodies, IGOs compile and publish many of the major research sources in international law.

a. *United Nations and Related Agencies*

The United Nations, founded in 1945 as a successor to the League of Nations, has influenced the development of international law by providing an organizational forum and a center for the preparation and promotion of legislation and conventions. Its five principal organs are the General Assembly, Security Council, Economic and Social Council, Secretariat, and International Court of Justice (ICJ).

The United Nations website (www.un.org) has a wealth of information about the organization, including news, descriptive overviews of its activities, and access to numerous documents. One of the best sources for basic information is *United Nations*

Handbook, published annually in print and online by the New Zealand Ministry of Foreign Affairs and Trade (www.mfat.govt.nz). More extensive commentaries include *The Charter of the United Nations: A Commentary* (Bruno Simma et al eds., 3d ed. 2012) and *The Oxford Handbook on the United Nations* (Thomas G. Weiss & Sam Daws eds., 2007). *Max Planck Yearbook of United Nations Law* (1997–date) (www.mpfpr.de/publications/) is a major source for current scholarly commentary; most volumes are available free online.

The *Yearbook of the United Nations* (unyearbook.un.org) is a good starting point for historical research on UN activities. Although coverage is delayed three or four years, this publication summarizes major developments, reprints major documents, and provides references to other sources for the year covered. The website has retrospective coverage from the first volume in 1946.

General Assembly Official Records (GAOR) has transcripts of the meetings of the assembly and its committees, accompanied by *Annexes* (important documents produced during the session) and *Supplements* (annual reports submitted by the Secretary-General, Security Council, International Court of Justice, and various committees). The final supplement each year is a compilation of the resolutions passed by the General Assembly.

Resolutions are also reprinted in the *Yearbook of the United Nations* and are available online. The Official Document System of the United Nations (documents.un.org) has the searchable full text of all resolutions since 1946 and other documents beginning in 1993.

The UN produces a broad range of other publications, including specialized yearbooks, statistical compilations, and conference proceedings. UN publications are indexed in UNBISNET: United Nations Bibliographic Information System (unbisnet. un.org). Access UN (www.readex.com) has comprehensive retrospective coverage.

HeinOnline's United Nations Law Collection has an array of U.N. legal publications, including resolutions, yearbooks, treaty publications, ICJ and ITLOS decisions, UNCITRAL documents, *Reports of International Arbitral Awards*, and several other works.

The United Nations also coordinates the work of several "specialized agencies" in particular subject fields, such as the Food and Agriculture Organization, the International Labour Organisation, and the World Health Organization. The United Nations System website (www.unsceb.org) has a directory with links to sites for more than eighty specialized organizations.

The U.N.'s Dag Hammarskjöld Library has published more than three dozen research guides on its website (research.un.org), some explaining the major organizational units and others focusing on specific topics such as the environment, health, human rights, or international law.

b. World Trade Organization

The World Trade Organization (www.wto.org) was established in 1995 as the principal international body administering trade agreements among member states. The WTO acts as a forum for negotiations, seeks to resolve disputes, and oversees national trade policies. Basic documents governing WTO operations are available on its website, and its *Annual Report* provides trade statistics and a commentary on the organization's work every year.

Controversies among WTO members are resolved by the Dispute Settlement Body. A three-member panel makes findings of fact and conclusions, and its report is subject to review by the Appellate Body. Panel decisions and Appellate Body reports are available in the "Trade Topics: Dispute Settlement" section of the WTO website as well as in several commercial series, including *International Trade Law Reports* and *World Trade Organization Dispute Settlement Decisions: Bernan's Annotated Reporter*, and on Westlaw and Lexis. WorldTradeLaw.net has summaries and texts of decisions as well as other WTO documents. Commentaries on the WTO include Mitsuo Matsushita et al., *The World Trade Organization: Law, Practice, and Policy* (3d ed. 2015).

c. European Union and Other Regional Organizations

For American lawyers, the European Union (europa.eu) is probably the most frequently encountered of the world's many regional organizations. The EU was established in 1993 by the Treaty on

European Union (the Maastricht Treaty) as the more ambitious successor to the European Communities (European Atomic Energy Community, European Coal and Steel Community, and European Economic Community). As economic and social developments have led to increasing European integration and the Treaty on European Union has been amended by the Treaty of Lisbon (2007), the EU is sometimes seen more as a supranational government than as a regional organization.

The major institutions of the EU are the European Commission, which proposes legislation, implements policies, and manages the Union; the European Parliament, a large elected body with legislative and advisory functions; the Council, which coordinates economic policies, concludes international agreements, and legislates in conjunction with the European Parliament; and the European Court of Justice (discussed earlier with other regional courts). The EU legislates through *regulations*, which are directly binding and don't require implementing legislation in member states, and *directives*, which must be implemented by member states to become effective.

Legislation and major documents are published in the EU's twenty-four official languages. The *Official Journal of the European Union* consists of two series, *Legislation* (L) and *Information and Notices* (C), and is available through EUR-Lex (eur-lex.europa.eu), along with a Directory of European Union Legislation in Force that provides subject access to treaties, regulations, directives, and other legislative actions.

Westlaw and Lexis also have extensive EU collections. In addition to primary sources, Lexis has the four-volume treatise *Smit & Herzog on the Law of the European Union* (2d ed. 2005–date).

Several other reference sources on EU law are published. *Encyclopedia of European Union Law: Constitutional Texts* has annotated versions of the treaties and other major texts, and *European Union Law Reporter* has broad coverage of documents and analysis. One-volume works include Ralph H. Folsom, *Principles of European Union Law* (4th ed. 2014) and P.S.R.F. Mathijsen, *A Guide to European Union Law* (10th ed. 2010).

Other important regional organizations include the African Union (www.au.int), Council of Europe (www.coe.int), and Organization of American States (OAS) (www.oas.org), all of which draft and promote multilateral treaties among their member states. As discussed earlier, they also have judicial systems designed to protect human rights in their regions.

Information on about thirty major intergovernmental organizations can be found in *International Encyclopaedia of Laws: Intergovernmental Organizations* (www.kluwerlawonline.com).

Non-governmental organizations (NGOs) such as Amnesty International or Greenpeace can be important sources of information, through their websites and their publications, in areas such as human rights or international environmental law. The *Yearbook of International Organizations* (www.uia.be/yearbook) is a six-volume directory with profiles and contact information for thousands of international groups and associations.

§ 9–7.   Sources for Further Information

Bibliographies and research guides can be invaluable sources of leads and research tips for the wide range of print and electronic sources in international law. The American Society of International Law's ASIL Electronic Resource Guide (www.asil. org/erg/) is useful and frequently updated. It has narrative descriptions of and links to resources on treaties, international organizations (as well as chapters on the European Union and the United Nations), and several topical areas such as human rights, environmental law, and intellectual property. Another major Internet source for international law information is GlobaLex (www.nyulawglobal.org/ globalex/), which publishes several dozen research guides on specific topics, each containing numerous links to resources.

Marci Hoffman & Mary Rumsey, *International and Foreign Legal Research: A Coursebook* (2d ed. 2012) and Anthony S. Winer et al., *International Law Legal Research* (2013) are thorough examinations of research methods, generally and in several special-ized areas. The George Washington International Law Review's annual *Guide to International Legal Research*, available on Lexis, has annotated listings of published and online resources.

CHAPTER 10

THE LAW OF OTHER COUNTRIES

Images of some resources discussed in this chapter are at **libguides.law.virginia.edu/nutshell12/ch10**

---

§ 10–1. Introduction

Globalization has made the laws of other countries increasingly significant to American social, economic and legal life. The law of a foreign country may be relevant in U.S. court proceedings involving family law or international trade, and scholars and lawmakers study other legal systems to better understand and improve our own. Any American lawyer dealing with a transnational matter must know how to develop a basic understanding of the other country's law.

Foreign law sources are also essential to the study of comparative law, in which differences among national legal systems are analyzed. The extent to which American courts should cite precedent from other countries is the subject of vigorous debate, but there is no question that decisions from common law countries have had persuasive value in the development of American jurisprudence.

§ 10–2.   Legal Systems of the World

The legal systems of most countries are classified as either *common law* or *civil law*. Each system has its own history, fundamental principles, procedures, and forms of publication for legal sources. As explained in Chapter 1, legal doctrine under the common law is traditionally developed over time through specific cases decided by judges rather than from broad, abstract codifications. Judicial decisions are among the most important sources of new legal rules in a common law system.

Civil law is derived from Roman law, and forms the basis for the legal systems of the countries of continental Europe, Latin America, and parts of Africa and Asia. The civil law system has several distinctive characteristics, including the predominance of comprehensive and systematic codes governing large fields of law, little weight allocated to judicial decisions as legal authority, and great influence of legal scholars who interpret, criticize and develop the law through commentaries on the codes.

Some jurisdictions do not fit clearly into either major system. A few countries, such as Scotland and

South Africa, have aspects of both civil law and common law. Others are strongly influenced by customary law or traditional religious systems, particularly Islamic or Talmudic law. Some countries combine elements of three or more legal systems.

JuriGlobe (www.juriglobe.ca) is an online guide with maps, descriptions of the major systems, and lists of countries in each category. Texts discussing the history and concepts of the world's legal systems include H. Patrick Glenn, *Legal Traditions of the World: Sustainable Diversity in Law* (5th ed. 2014); John W. Head, *Great Legal Traditions: Civil Law, Common Law, and Chinese Law in Historical and Operational Perspective* (2011); and Thomas Lundmark, *Charting the Divide Between Common and Civil Law* (2012).

The differences between the common law and civil law systems have become less marked in recent years, as each system adopts features of the other. American jurisdictions have increasingly enacted comprehensive subject codifications, such as the Uniform Commercial Code, while some civil law countries are giving greater weight to judicial decisions. Nonetheless, basic differences remain in how legal issues are perceived and how research is conducted.

§ 10–3. Reference Resources

While thorough research on a foreign law issue requires you to read the original primary sources, you can develop a working knowledge of major legal issues through print and online reference materials.

You will usually want to begin with an encyclopedia or treatise for a general introduction to a national legal system or a specific subject, and then find translations or summaries of the primary sources. Foreign law research guides describing and linking to sources can help you discover the available resources.

a. Encyclopedias and Legal System Guides

Several encyclopedic works discuss national legal systems and specific legal topics within those systems.

Legal Systems of the World: A Political, Social, and Cultural Encyclopedia (Herbert M. Kritzer ed., 2002) is a four-volume work providing an introductory overview by jurisdiction and subject. Its articles on countries discuss their history, major legal concepts, and the structure of the legal system, with references for further reading. Its subject articles generally compare civil law and common law approaches.

The Oxford International Encyclopedia of Legal History (Stanley N. Katz ed., 2009) is a six-volume set with more than 1,000 articles on a wide range of legal topics in ancient, medieval, and modern legal systems. Articles include cross-references and bibliographies.

The United States government publishes several guides to legal issues in foreign countries. The International Trade Administration's Export.gov website (www.export.gov/mrktresearch/) has legal and commercial guides for specific countries and industries. The Department of State's Bureau of Consular Affairs (travel.state.gov) has a "Legal Considerations" page, part of which covers International Judicial Assistance topics such as enforcement of judgments and obtaining evidence abroad.

The Central Intelligence Agency's *World Factbook* (www.cia.gov) has demographic and economic information about the countries of the world. Basic country information, such as economic conditions, political developments, and statistics, can also be found in reference sources such as *Europa World Year Book* (www.europaworld.com) and *The Statesman's Yearbook* (www.statesmansyearbook. com). *Law and Judicial Systems of Nations* (4th ed. 2002) has a concise overview of bar organization, legal education, and court systems of 193 countries, with a brief explanation of each legal system.

A number of guides to the legal systems of specific countries are published in English. These generally explain legal institutions, summarize major principles, and have leads to research resources. Recently published titles include Michael A. Livingston et al., *The Italian Legal System: An Introduction* (2015) and Husnu Al Suood, *The Maldivian Legal System* (2014). Some works cover the legal systems of a region, such as *Mixed Legal Systems, East and West* (Vernon Valentine Palmer et al. eds., 2015).

The most comprehensive treatment of comparative law is the *International Encyclopedia of Comparative Law* (1971–date). Of seventeen planned volumes, only eight have been published in their final bound format. Pamphlets on specific topics have been issued in other areas, including a series of "National Reports" pamphlets on individual countries.

Three one-volume reference works have more current coverage of comparative law issues. *The Cambridge Companion to Comparative Law* (Mauro Bussani & Ugo Mattei eds., 2012), *Elgar Encyclopedia of Comparative Law* (Jan M. Smits ed., 2d ed. 2012), and *The Oxford Handbook of Comparative Law* (Mathias Reimann & Reinhard Zimmermann eds., 2006) all contain chapters by leading scholars analyzing various legal traditions as well as studies of particular topics and subject areas.

International Encyclopaedia of Laws (*IEL*) (www.kluwerlawonline.com) consists of about two dozen sets focusing on specific subjects such as civil procedure, cyber law, or medical law. Each subject set has separate monographic pamphlets for individual countries.

b. Research Guides and Indexes

When starting research in the law of another country, you need a sense of its major primary sources and the places where you can find answers and analysis. A research guide can point the way and make you a knowledgeable traveler in a foreign land.

Foreign Law Guide (referenceworks.brillonline.com) is one of the best starting points, covering almost every country in the world. It discusses each national legal system and its history, describes the major codifications and gazettes, notes sources for legislation and court decisions (including those available in English), and lists codes and laws covering specific subject areas. Links are provided to sources available online.

GlobaLex (www.nyulawglobal.org/globalex/) is a free website with research guides for more than 150 countries. These guides summarize the legal system and describe available documentation, with links to numerous web resources.

Research in foreign legal systems generally is discussed in Marci Hoffman & Mary Rumsey's *International and Foreign Legal Research: A Coursebook* (2d ed. 2012). English legal research is covered by John Knowles, *Effective Legal Research* (3d ed. 2012); and similar treatment for Canada is offered by works such as Nancy McCormack et al., *The Practical Guide to Canadian Legal Research* (4th ed. 2015).

Articles on foreign legal issues can be found in the legal periodical databases and indexes discussed in Chapter 2. Deeper coverage is available from specialized resources. *Index to Foreign Legal Periodicals*, available through HeinOnline, covers more than 500 journals from seventy-five countries, as well as commemorative *festschriften* and other collections of essays. It indexes journals published outside the United States, the United Kingdom, and the Commonwealth, and articles in selected American and Commonwealth journals on international law, comparative law, or the domestic law of other countries. Westlaw has *Legal Journals Index*, which covers more than 800 British and European publications.

c. Summaries and Translations of Laws

If you are relying on English-language sources in your research, you can find summaries and analyses of foreign laws as well as some translations of legal texts. While summaries and translations are not substitutes for the original sources, they can familiarize you with the basic concepts and issues of a foreign law problem.

The basic laws of government structure and individual liberties are found in national constitutions. Two works with introductory overviews are *Encyclopedia of World Constitutions* (Gerhard Robbers ed., 2007) and Robert L. Maddex, *Constitutions of the World* (3d ed. 2008). Each summarizes the constitutional histories, governmental structures, and approaches to fundamental rights of more than 100 countries. Broader scholarly treatment of major themes is available in *Comparative Constitutional Law* (Tom Ginsburg & Rosalind Dixon eds., 2011) and *The Oxford Handbook of Comparative Constitutional Law* (Michel Rosenfeld & András Sajó eds., 2012).

Thorough coverage of current national constitutions is available from two online resources, HeinOnline's World Constitutions Illustrated and Oxford Constitutions of the World (oxcon.ouplaw. com). HeinOnline has texts in the original language and, where available, in English, and accompanies each set of constitutional documents with relevant treatises and journal articles as well as bibliographies of other commentaries. The Oxford resource, available in print as *Constitutions of the Countries of the World* (1971–date), has English translations of all documents, and includes bibliographies and constitutional overviews as well. Free online resources include Constitute (www.constituteproject.org) and the University of Richmond's Constitution Finder (confinder.richmond.edu).

Horst Dippel of the University of Kassel has assembled two comprehensive collections of historic constitutions. *Constitutions of the World, 1850 to the Present* (2002–date) is a set of modern constitutions on microfiche, and *Constitutions of the World from the Late 18th Century to the Middle of the 19th Century* (2005–date) (www.modern-constitutions.de) is a print and online compilation of historic sources.

Codes and statutes are far less likely than constitutions to be found in translation. Legifrance (www.legifrance.gouv.fr) has English translations of major French codes, and the German Law Archive (www.iuscomp.org/gla/) has numerous sources in English including statutes, court decisions, and secondary sources.

Laws affecting international business are the most likely statutes to be available in English. Several collections covering specific topics are published, including *Digest of Commercial Laws of the World* and *International Securities Regulation*, both of which are available online under some Westlaw subscriptions. Getting the Deal Through (getting thedealthrough.com), available in Bloomberg Law's "Books & Treatises" collection, has concise explanations of national laws in more than 70 business-related practice areas.

Online collections of national laws in specific subject areas are available from several international organizations. These include the International Labour Organization's NATLEX (natlex.ilo.org), UNESCO's Collection of National Copyright Laws (www.unesco.org/culture/copy/), and the World Intellectual Property Organization's WipoLex (www.wipo.int/wipolex/).

Relatively few judicial decisions in foreign languages are translated into English, but possible resources include *International Law Reports*, with cases from national courts on international law and human rights topics, and the University of Texas's Foreign Law Translations site (law.utexas.edu/transnational/), with decisions from Austria, France, Germany, and Israel. Specialized publications include *Bulletin on Constitutional Case-Law* (www.codices.coe.int), *East European Case Reporter of Constitutional Law*, and *International Labour Law Reports* (available on HeinOnline).

While it cannot substitute for professional translation, an automated translation service such as Google Translate (translate.google.com) can give you at least a sense of the scope and subject of a document. This may help you determine whether a more accurate translation is needed.

d. Dictionaries

Language differences can be a major hurdle to understanding legal sources from a foreign legal system. Even legal systems sharing the same language can have different meanings for the same terms. Legal dictionaries can give you at least a superficial sense of the differences in meaning and usage.

The major British legal dictionary is *Jowitt's Dictionary of English Law* (4th ed. 2015); two shorter paperback works are *The Law Student's Dictionary* (2008) and *Osborn's Concise Law Dictionary* (12th ed. 2013). The *Dictionary of Canadian Law* (4th ed. 2011) is the most substantial treatment of Canadian legal definitions.

Numerous bilingual dictionaries translate foreign terms into English, although many of these simply translate words without explaining the underlying legal concepts. Two recommended works by Henry Saint Dahl, with definitions derived from statutes and other primary sources, are *Dahl's Law Dictionary: Spanish-English/English-Spanish* (5th ed. 2010) and *Dahl's Law Dictionary: French to English/English to French* (3d ed. 2007). Other respected Spanish/English dictionaries include *Merl Bilingual Law Dictionary* (2005), and *Mexican Legal Dictionary* (2012 ed.).

Citation forms for foreign legal materials are often confusing for American lawyers. *The Bluebook* includes information for more than forty countries, covering statutory, judicial, and other frequently cited sources. Broader coverage is provided by *Guide to Foreign and International Legal Citations* (2d ed. 2009). Guides to citation format in other countries include *OSCOLA: Oxford University Standard for Citation of Legal Authorities* (4th ed. 2012) (www. law.ox.ac.uk/oscola) and the McGill Law Journal's

Canadian Guide to Uniform Legal Citation (8th ed. 2014). *World Dictionary of Legal Abbreviations* (1991–date) has lists of foreign abbreviations, with separate sections for some two dozen countries, languages, regions, and subjects.

§ 10–4. Original Sources

Your next step after consulting available reference materials is to investigate primary legal sources from the country. Many of these sources are available online, although understanding them still requires knowledge of a foreign legal system and its language. Many countries have both free and subscription-based services similar to those available in the United States. This section focuses on resources available to most American researchers.

a. Links to Country Websites

Several resources provide access to law-related websites in countries around the world. Foreign Law Guide (www.foreignlawguide.com) and GlobaLex (www.nyulawglobalaw.org/globalex/), both discussed earlier, combine descriptive summaries with links to sources. The World Bank's Doing Business site (www.doingbusiness.org/law-library/) has links to national laws on business-related topics for more than 180 countries.

Other sites with country pages and links to consti-tutions, legislation, government sites, and other resources include the Library of Congress's Guide to Law Online (www.loc.gov/law/help/guide.php) and the World Legal Information Institute (WorldLII) (www.worldlii.org). Many academic law library websites also feature guides with links to foreign law sources.

b. Common Law Jurisdictions

The resources and research methods for common law countries are similar to those of the United States. This section looks briefly at two of our most closely related common law jurisdictions: England (which is part of the United Kingdom but has a separate body of law from Northern Ireland and Scotland) and Canada. Similar resources are available for other common law countries such as Australia and New Zealand.

The United Kingdom has an "unwritten" constitution, meaning that its basic constitutional principles are not found in one specific document. One major difference between British and U.S. law is that the U.K. Parliament has unlimited power, and its acts cannot be held unconstitutional. Canada's Constitution, dating to 1867, is the source of powers for both the federal Parliament and the provincial legislatures. Areas such as criminal law and family law are matters of Canadian federal law rather than provincial law, and in general any powers not expressly delegated to the provinces are reserved to the federal government.

Case Law. Judicial decisions from other common law countries can have persuasive value in U.S. courts and are thus valuable primary sources for American lawyers. Even more significant are the historical cases predating U.S. independence that were expressly accepted by state reception statutes as part of American common law.

English law reporting dates back to the fragmentary reports in the *Plea Rolls*, beginning with the reign of Richard I in 1189. The *Year Books*, covering 1285 to 1537, contain notes of debates between judges and counsel on the points in issue in cases. Following the *Year Books* for several centuries came the *nominate* or *nominative* reports, that is, court reports named for the person who recorded or edited them.

More than 270 series of nominative reports were cumulated into *The English Reports* (1900–32), covering cases from 1220 to 1865 in 176 volumes. *The English Reports* is available online from several subscription sources, including Westlaw and HeinOnline, and free from the Commonwealth Legal Information Institute (www.commonlii.org/uk/cases/ EngR/). Another compilation of older cases, the *Revised Reports*, includes some decisions not found in *The English Reports*. The leading source for accounts of major trials for treason and related offenses is *A Complete Collection of State Trials* (William Cobbett & Thomas Bayly Howell eds., 1809–28; in HeinOnline's World Trials Library).

The modern English judicial system has replaced a complex collection of specialized courts with a more straightforward structure of trial and appellate courts. Civil actions are tried in one of the divisions of the High Court (Queen's Bench, Chancery, or Family) or in lower courts of limited jurisdiction, with review by the Court of Appeal and from there by the

Supreme Court, which replaced the House of Lords as the court of last resort in 2009. Criminal trials are conducted in a Crown Court, with the same two-tier appeal system.

The Canadian court system is similar to that of the United States, with federal and provincial courts, although the Supreme Court of Canada is the final arbiter on both federal and provincial issues. Most matters are first heard in provincial court, but the Federal Court of Canada has trial jurisdiction over matters such as intellectual property, maritime law, and claims against the government.

As in the United States, new British and Canadian decisions are published in official or authorized series of reports and in unofficial commercial reporters and online services. Westlaw and Lexis have broad coverage of judicial decisions from both countries. Free Internet access to decisions is provided by the British and Irish Legal Information Institute (BAILII) (www.bailii.org) and the Canadian Legal Information Institute (CanLII) (www.canlii.org). The British site JustisOne (one.justis.org) has case law since 1855, with free access to decisions since 2001.

The standard source for modern English decisions is the semi-official *Law Reports* (1865–date), which now consists of four series: *Appeal Cases* (Supreme Court, European Court of Justice, and Judicial Committee of the Privy Council), *Queen's Bench Division*; *Chancery Division*; and *Family Division*. *All England Law Reports* (1936–date) is a commercially published reporter and includes some decisions not found in the official series.

Canada has authorized reports for its federal courts (*Canada Supreme Court Reports* and *Federal Court Reports*), as well as reports for provincial and territorial courts, unofficial series such as *Dominion Law Reports*, and a variety of specialized topical reporters.

Halsbury's Laws of England is the standard English encyclopedia, encompassing statutes and administrative sources as well as case law. A similar Canadian publication, *Halsbury's Laws of Canada*, began in 2006 and was recently completed. Two regional encyclopedias, both of which include coverage of Canadian federal law, are *Canadian Encyclopedic Digest (Ontario)* (4th ed. 2009–date), and *Canadian Encyclopedic Digest (Western)* (4th ed. 2009–date). These are available as one work on Westlaw, along with several dozen Canadian treatises.

Both England and Canada have major national digests, somewhat similar to the West digest system: *The Digest: Annotated British, Commonwealth and European Cases* and the *Canadian Abridgment*. Each country also has tools for finding later cases that have considered an earlier decision, such as *Current Law Case Citator* in England and *Canadian Case Citations*. Westlaw includes citing references for Canadian cases.

Statutes. Legislation in other common law jurisdictions is published both in session laws and in compilations of statutes in force, available from government and commercial websites. One major difference from the U.S. model is that statutes are generally compiled alphabetically or chronologically, rather than by subject as in the *United States Code*. Statutes are not assigned code titles and sections, but instead are usually identified by their original name and date of enactment.

The most frequently used printed source for English statutes is the unofficial compilation *Halsbury's Statutes of England and Wales*. This is somewhat similar to U.S. annotated codes in that sections are followed by footnote summaries of judicial decisions. Current United Kingdom statutes and regulations (known as *statutory instruments*) are available free from the U.K. National Archives (legislation.gov.uk) as well as through Westlaw and other services.

For Canadian statutes there is no annotated, regularly updated publication similar to *Halsbury's Statutes*. Federal statutes and regulations are available from the Department of Justice (laws-lois.justice.gc.ca), and CanLII (www.canlii.org) has links to provincial sources. Westlaw also has federal and provincial statutes, accompanied by citing references.

The standard historical collection of English statutes is the *Statutes of the Realm* (1810–28, covering 1235 to 1714), in HeinOnline's English Reports Library. Several other chronological collections were published during the 19th century under the title *Statutes at Large*, extending coverage to the beginning of the modern *Public General Acts* in 1866. JustisOne has subscription online coverage of statutes from 1235 to date.

The first step in identifying and finding an older English statute is deciphering its citation. Acts before 1963 are generally cited not by calendar year but by regnal year (the year of a monarch's rule). The act that changed the citation system, for example, was passed during the session of Parliament that spanned the tenth and eleventh years of the reign of Elizabeth II, and is cited as Acts of Parliament Numbering and Citation Act, 10 & 11 Eliz. 2, ch. 34 (1962). Tables to convert regnal years to calendar years are printed in reference works such as *Black's Law Dictionary*, and regnal year calculators are available online.

c. Civil Law Jurisdictions

An American lawyer or law student researching the law of a civil law country must be cognizant of the major differences between the civil and common law systems, and the effect of these differences on how legal problems are evaluated and researched. In theory, a code in the civil law tradition is designed to cover all legal situations that might occur. Instead of searching for precedents in factually similar judicial decisions, as a civil law researcher you would look first to the abstract provisions of the code for a logical and appropriate legal principle.

Secondary sources are invaluable in civil law research. Scholarly commentary is given great weight by civil lawyers, and leading treatises are essential resources. Some legal encyclopedias, particularly the French *répertoires* published by Dalloz, are also highly esteemed, with articles by leading legal scholars.

Civil law countries also have a multitude of legal periodicals commenting on legal developments and often printing legislative texts and judicial decisions. In France, for example, the leading legal periodicals *Recueil Dalloz* and *La Semaine Juridique* provide both primary sources and scholarly articles.

After introductory study in an encyclopedia, treatise, or journal article, your next step is to consult the relevant code or other statutes applicable to the problem. Most civil law countries have several separately published codes. These include the traditional major codes (civil, criminal, commercial, civil procedure and criminal procedure), and more recent codifications compiling statutes on specific subjects such as taxation, labor law, and family law.

Some civil law countries, such as France, rely primarily on annotated editions of the codes. In others, particularly Germany, exhaustive article-by-article commentaries on the major codes are among the most important legal sources. The most scholarly of these commentaries, such as the one-volume *Palandt* and the multivolume *Staudinger*, have considerable persuasive authority, often greater than judicial decisions.

Official websites in many countries provide access to their codes, although these versions rarely include annotations or commentary. Westlaw and Lexis have primary sources from very few jurisdictions in their original language, but foreign subscription services (if available) offer more extensive coverage.

After studying the code and commentary, you should then find administrative orders and judicial decisions implementing or interpreting the legislative norms. Legislation, regulations, and decrees are most often found in official gazettes, comparable to but usually broader in scope than the *Federal Register*. Foreign Law Guide lists these sources, with links where available.

Court decisions are published in most civil law countries, even though they are generally of secondary importance. Their status is gradually changing, in part because civil lawyers now study precedent from supranational bodies such as the European Court of Justice and the World Trade Organization. Most civil law jurisdictions, however, continue to have fewer court reports and less developed tools for finding cases by subject. In many countries, you may need to search legal periodicals for relevant court decisions. Sources such as the Foreign Law Guide and Globalex articles list appropriate sources.

APPENDIX A
STATE LEGAL RESEARCH GUIDES

These guides are suggested for further information on the materials and research methods in individual states. The list is limited to works published since 2000, and includes numerous chapters discussing state practice materials and research methods in a two-volume looseleaf set edited by Frank G. Houdek, *State Practice Materials: Annotated Bibliographies* (2002–date) (available on HeinOnline in Spinelli's Law Library Reference Shelf). The American Association of Law Libraries has issued a series of brief bibliographies of state government documents, which are not listed here but are accessible in HeinOnline as well. Websites for law libraries within a state are also good sources for guides listing and describing the state's major printed and online legal resources.

Alabama

Gary Orlando Lewis, *Legal Research in Alabama* (2001).

Scott DeLeve, "Alabama Practice Materials: A Selective Annotated Bibliography" (2005), in 1 *State Practice Materials: Annotated Bibliographies.*

Alaska

Catherine Lemann & Susan Falk, "Alaska Practice Materials: A Selective Annotated Bibliography" (2008), in 1 *State Practice Materials: Annotated Bibliographies.*

Arizona

Tamara S. Herrera, *Arizona Legal Research* (2d ed. 2013).

Jacquelyne Gayle Kasper, "Arizona Practice Materials: A Selective Annotated Bibliography" (2009), in 1 *State Practice Materials: Annotated Bibliographies.*

Arkansas

Coleen M. Barger, *Arkansas Legal Research* (2007).

Kathryn C. Fitzhugh et al., "Arkansas Practice Materials: A Selective Annotated Bibliography" (2013), in 1 *State Practice Materials: Annotated Bibliographies.*

California

Larry D. Dershem, *California Legal Research Handbook* (2d ed. 2008).

John K. Hanft, *Legal Research in California* (7th ed. 2011).

Henke's California Law Guide (Daniel W. Martin ed., 8th ed. 2006).

Judy C. Janes, "California Practice Materials: A Selective Annotated Bibliography" (2005), in 1 *State Practice Materials: Annotated Bibliographies.*

Hether C. Macfarlane et al., *California Legal Research* (2d ed. 2013).

Colorado

Mitch Fontenot, "Colorado Practice Materials: A Selective Annotated Bibliography" (2004), in 1 *State Practice Materials: Annotated Bibliographies.*

Robert Michael Linz, *Colorado Legal Research* (2010).

Connecticut

M. Caitlin S. Anderson & Lee Sims, "Connecticut Practice Materials: A Selective Annotated Bibliography" (2009), in 1 *State Practice Materials: Annotated Bibliographies.*

Jessica G. Hynes, *Connecticut Legal Research* (2009).

District of Columbia

Leah F. Chanin, "Legal Research in the District of Columbia," in *Legal Research in the District of Columbia, Maryland and Virginia* (2d ed. 2000).

Michelle Wu, "District of Columbia Practice Materials: A Selective Annotated Bibliography" (2002), in 1 *State Practice Materials: Annotated Bibliographies.*

Florida

Barbara J. Busharis et al., *Florida Legal Research* (4th ed. 2014).

Nancy L. Strohmeyer, "Florida Practice Materials: A Selective Annotated Bibliography" (2d ed. 2013), in 1 *State Practice Materials: Annotated Bibliographies.*

Betsy L. Stupski, *Guide to Florida Legal Research* (7th ed. 2008).

Georgia

Nancy P. Johnson et al., *Georgia Legal Research* (2007).

Austin Martin Williams et al., "Georgia Practice Materials: A Selective Annotated Bibliography" (3d ed.

2014), in 1 *State Practice Materials: Annotated Bibliographies*.

Hawai'i

Leina'ala R. Seeger, "Hawaii Practice Materials: A Selective Annotated Bibliography" (2004), in 1 *State Practice Materials: Annotated Bibliographies*.

Idaho

Tenielle Fordyce-Ruff & Kristina Running, *Idaho Legal Research* (2d ed. 2015).

Jean Mattimoe, "Idaho Practice Materials: A Selective Annotated Bibliography" (2009), in 1 *State Practice Materials: Annotated Bibliographies*.

Illinois

Phill W. Johnson, "Illinois Practice Materials: A Selective Annotated Bibliography" (2006), in 1 *State Practice Materials: Annotated Bibliographies*.

Laurel Wendt, *Illinois Legal Research Guide* (2d ed. 2006).

Mark E. Wojcik, *Illinois Legal Research* (2d ed. 2009).

Indiana

Richard E. Humphrey, "Indiana Practice Materials: A Selective Annotated Bibliography" (2004), in 1 *State Practice Materials: Annotated Bibliographies*.

Iowa

John D. Edwards et al., *Iowa Legal Research* (2011).

Iowa Legal Research Guide (John D. Edwards ed., 2003).

Kansas

Joseph A. Custer & Christopher L. Steadham, *Kansas Legal Research* (2008).

Joseph A. Custer et al., *Kansas Legal Research and Reference Guide* (3d ed. 2003).

Joseph A. Custer, "Kansas Practice Materials: A Selective Annotated Bibliography" (2002), in 1 *State Practice Materials: Annotated Bibliographies.*

Kentucky

Helane E. Davis, "Kentucky Practice Materials: A Selective Annotated Bibliography" (2009), in 1 *State Practice Materials: Annotated Bibliographies.*

William A. Hilyerd et al., *Kentucky Legal Research* (2012).

Kurt X. Metzmeier et al., *Kentucky Legal Research Manual* (3d ed. 2005).

Louisiana

Mary Garvey Algero, *Louisiana Legal Research* (2d ed. 2013).

Catherine Lemann, "Louisiana Practice Materials: A Selective Annotated Bibliography" (2006), in 1 *State Practice Materials: Annotated Bibliographies.*

Maryland

Khelani Clay & Adeen Postar, "Maryland Practice Materials: A Selective Annotated Bibliography" (2011), in 1 *State Practice Materials: Annotated Bibliographies.*

Pamela J. Gregory, "Legal Research in Maryland," in *Legal Research in the District of Columbia, Maryland and Virginia* (2d ed. 2000).

Massachusetts

E. Joan Blum, *Massachusetts Legal Research* (2010).

Handbook of Legal Research in Massachusetts (Mary Ann Neary ed., 3d ed. 2009).

Michigan

Pamela Lysaght & Cristina D. Lockwood, *Michigan Legal Research* (2d ed. 2011).

Minnesota

Vicente E. Garces, "Minnesota Practice Materials: A Selective Annotated Bibliography" (2002), in 1 *State Practice Materials: Annotated Bibliographies*.

John Tessner et al., *Minnesota Legal Research Guide* (2d ed. 2002).

Suzanne Thorpe, *Minnesota Legal Research* (2010).

Mississippi

Anne M. Klingen, "Mississippi Practice Materials: A Selective Annotated Bibliography" (2002), in 1 *State Practice Materials: Annotated Bibliographies*.

Kristy L. Gilliland, *Mississippi Legal Research* (2014).

Missouri

Wanda M. Temm & Julie M. Cheslik, *Missouri Legal Research* (3d ed. 2015).

Montana

Robert K. Whelan et al., *A Guide to Montana Legal Research* (8th ed. 2003) (courts.mt.gov/portals/113/library/guides/guide.pdf).

Nebraska

Kay L. Andrus et al., *Research Guide to Nebraska Law* (2008 ed.).

Beth Smith, "Nebraska Practice Materials: A Selective Annotated Bibliography" (2004), in 2 *State Practice Materials: Annotated Bibliographies*.

Nevada

Nevada Legal Research Guide (Jennifer Larraguibel Gross & Thomas Blake Gross eds., 2012).

New Jersey

Paul Axel-Lute, *New Jersey Legal Research Handbook* (6th ed. 2012).

David A. Hollander, "New Jersey Practice Materials: A Selective Annotated Bibliography" (2008), in 2 *State Practice Materials: Annotated Bibliographies*.

New Mexico

Ripple L. Weistling, "New Mexico Practice Materials: A Selective Annotated Bibliography" (2010), in 2 *State Practice Materials: Annotated Bibliographies*.

New York

Elizabeth G. Adelman et al., *New York Legal Research* (3d ed. 2015).

William H. Manz, *Gibson's New York Legal Research Guide* (4th ed. 2014).

William Manz, "New York Practice Materials: A Selective Annotated Bibliography" (2009), in 2 *State Practice Materials: Annotated Bibliographies*.

North Carolina

Miriam J. Baer & James C. Ray, *Legal Research in North Carolina* (2006).

Scott Childs & Sara Sampson, *North Carolina Legal Research* (2d ed. 2014).

Scott Childs & Nick Sexton, *North Carolina Legal Research Guide* (2d ed. 2009).

Julie L. Kimbrough, "North Carolina Practice Materials: A Selective Annotated Bibliography" (2009), in 2 *State Practice Materials: Annotated Bibliographies*.

North Dakota

Rhonda R. Schwartz, "North Dakota Practice Materials: A Selective Annotated Bibliography" (2008), in 2 *State Practice Materials: Annotated Bibliographies*.

Ohio

Kenneth S. Kozlowski & Susan N. Elliott, "Ohio Practice Materials: A Selective Annotated Bibliography" (2005), in 2 *State Practice Materials: Annotated Bibliographies*.

Sara Sampson et al., *Ohio Legal Research* (2d ed. 2015).

Oklahoma

Darin K. Fox et al., *Oklahoma Legal Research* (2013).

Ann Walsh Long, "Oklahoma Practice Materials: A Selective Annotated Bibliography" (2007), in 2 *State Practice Materials: Annotated Bibliographies.*

Oregon

Mary Clayton & Stephanie Midkiff, "Oregon Practice Materials: A Selective Annotated Bibliography" (2005), in 2 *State Practice Materials: Annotated Bibliographies.*

Suzanne E. Rowe, *Oregon Legal Research* (3d ed. 2014).

Pennsylvania

Barbara J. Busharis & Bonny L. Tavares, *Pennsylvania Legal Research* (2007).

Joel Fishman & Marc Silverman, "Pennsylvania Practice Materials: A Selective Annotated Bibliography" (2003), in 2 *State Practice Materials: Annotated Bibliographies.*

Frank Y. Liu et al., *Pennsylvania Legal Research Handbook* (2008 ed.).

Puerto Rico

Luis Muñiz Argüelles et al., *La Investigación Jurídica: Fuentes Puertorriqueñas, Norteamericanas y Españolas* (5th ed. 2012).

Rhode Island

Daniel J. Donovan, *Legal Research in Rhode Island* (4th ed. 2004).

South Carolina

Paula Gail Benson & Deborah Davis Hottel, *A Guide to South Carolina Legal Research and Citation* (3d ed. 2014).

Pamela Rogers Melton & Christine L. Sellers, "South Carolina Practice Materials: A Selective Annotated Bibliography" (2d ed. 2011), in 2 *State Practice Materials: Annotated Bibliographies.*

South Dakota

Matthew E. Braun & Kasia Solon, "South Dakota Practice Materials: A Selective Annotated Bibliography" (2008), in 2 *State Practice Materials: Annotated Bibliographies.*

Tennessee

Toof Brown, III, "Tennessee Practice Materials: A Selective Annotated Bibliography" (2004), in 2 *State Practice Materials: Annotated Bibliographies.*

Sibyl Marshall & Carol McCrehan Parker, *Tennessee Legal Research* (2007).

Texas

Matthew C. Cordon & Brandon D. Quarles, *Specialized Topics in Texas Legal Research* (2005).

Brandon D. Quarles & Matthew C. Cordon, *Researching Texas Law* (3d ed. 2012).

Brandon D. Quarles & Matthew C. Cordon, "Texas Practice Materials: A Selective Annotated Bibliography" (2006), in 2 *State Practice Materials: Annotated Bibliographies.*

Spencer L. Simons, *Texas Legal Research* (rev. printing 2012).

Utah

Jessica Van Buren et al., *Utah Legal Research* (2011).

Virginia

A Guide to Legal Research in Virginia (John D. Eure & Gail F. Zwirner eds., 7th ed. 2012).

Leslie A. Lee, "Virginia Practice Materials: A Selective Annotated Bibliography" (2002), in 2 *State Practice Materials: Annotated Bibliographies.*

Sarah K. Wiant, "Legal Research in Virginia," in *Legal Research in the District of Columbia, Maryland and Virginia* (2d ed. 2000).

Washington

Penny A. Hazelton et al., *Washington Legal Researcher's Deskbook 3d* (2002).

Julie Heintz-Cho et al., *Washington Legal Research* (2d ed. 2009).

West Virginia

Ann Walsh Long, "West Virginia Practice Materials: A Selective Annotated Bibliography" (2004), in 2 *State Practice Materials: Annotated Bibliographies.*

Hollee Schwartz Temple, *West Virginia Legal Research* (2013).

Wisconsin

Patricia Cervenka & Leslie Behroozi, *Wisconsin Legal Research* (2011).

Legal Research in Wisconsin (Theodore A. Potter ed., 2d ed. 2008).

Julie A. Norton & Megan A. O'Brien, "Wisconsin Practice Materials: A Selective Annotated Bibliography" (2010), in 2 *State Practice Materials: Annotated Bibliographies.*

Wyoming

Debora A. Person & Tawnya K. Plumb, *Wyoming Legal Research* (2013).

Monica A. Sharum & Paul E. Howard, "Wyoming Practice Materials: A Selective Annotated Bibliography" (2004), in 2 *State Practice Materials: Annotated Bibliographies.*

APPENDIX B

MAJOR TREATISES AND SERVICES BY SUBJECT

ADMINISTRATIVE LAW (KF5401–KF5425)

Alfred C. Aman & William T. Mayton, *Administrative Law* (3d ed. 2014)

Charles H. Koch, Jr., *Administrative Law and Practice* (3d ed. 2010–date) [Westlaw]

Richard J. Pierce, Jr., *Administrative Law Treatise* (5th ed. 2010–date)

Jacob A. Stein et al., *Administrative Law* (1977–date) [Lexis]

ADMIRALTY AND MARITIME LAW (KF1096–KF1137)

Benedict on Admiralty (Joshua S. Force ed., 7th ed. 1958–date) [Lexis]

Thomas J. Schoenbaum, *Admiralty and Maritime Law* (5th ed. 2011–date) [Westlaw]

ANTITRUST & TRADE REGULATION (KF1601–KF1668)

Louis Altman & Malla Pollack, *Callmann on Unfair Competition, Trademarks and Monopolies* (4th ed. 1981–date) [Westlaw]

Philip Areeda & Herbert Hovenkamp, *Antitrust Law* (3d & 4th eds. 2006–date)

William C. Holmes, *Antitrust Law Handbook* (annual) [Westlaw]

Herbert Hovenkamp, *Federal Antitrust Policy: The Law of Competition and Its Practice* (5th ed. 2016)

Earl W. Kintner et al., *Federal Antitrust Law* (1st–3d eds. 1980–date) [Lexis]

Dee Pridgen & Richard M. Alderman, *Consumer Protection and the Law* (annual) [Westlaw]

Lawrence A. Sullivan et al., *The Law of Antitrust: An Integrated Handbook* (3d ed. 2016)

Julian O. Von Kalinowski et al., *Antitrust Laws and Trade Regulation* (2d ed. 1996–date) [Lexis]

Services: *Antitrust & Trade Regulation Report* (BNA), *Trade Regulation Reporter* (Wolters Kluwer)

ART AND ENTERTAINMENT LAW (KF4288–KF4305)

Alexandra Darraby, *Art, Artifact, Architecture and Museum Law* (annual) [Westlaw]

Ralph E. Lerner & Judith Bresler, *Art Law* (4th ed. 2012) [Bloomberg Law]

Alexander Lindey & Michael Landau, *Lindey on Entertainment, Publishing, and the Arts* (3d ed. 2004–date) [Westlaw]

BANKING AND CONSUMER FINANCE (KF966–KF1040)

Barkley Clark & Barbara Clark, *The Law of Bank Deposits, Collections, and Credit Cards* (3d ed. 2014–date) [Lexis, Westlaw]

Richard B. Hagedorn, *Brady on Bank Checks and Fund Transfers* (2012–date) [Lexis, Westlaw]

Michael P. Malloy, *Banking Law and Regulation* (2d ed. 2011–date)

Fred H. Miller & Alvin C. Harrell, *The Law of Modern Payment Systems* (2003)

Dee Pridgen & Richard M. Alderman, *Consumer Credit and the Law* (annual) [Westlaw]

William H. Schlichting et al., *Banking Law* (1981–date) [Lexis]

Services: *Banking Report* (BNA), *Consumer Credit Guide* (Wolters Kluwer), *Federal Banking Law Reporter* (Wolters Kluwer)

BANKRUPTCY (KF1501–KF1548)

Bloomberg Law: Bankruptcy Treatise (D. Michael Lynn et al. eds., 2014–date) [Bloomberg Law]

Collier on Bankruptcy (Alan N. Resnick & Henry J. Sommer eds., 16th ed. 2009–date) [Lexis]

Norton Bankruptcy Law and Practice (William L. Norton, Jr. & William L. Norton, III, eds., 3d ed. 2008–date) [Westlaw]

Henry J. Sommer, *Consumer Bankruptcy Law and Practice* (10th ed. 2012–date)

Charles Jordan Tabb, *The Law of Bankruptcy* (3d ed. 2014)

Services: *Bankruptcy Law Reporter* (BNA), *Bankruptcy Law Reporter* (Wolters Kluwer), *Bankruptcy Service* (West)

CHILDREN AND THE LAW (KF479, KF9771–KF9827)

Samuel M. Davis, *Rights of Juveniles: The Juvenile Justice System* (annual) [Westlaw]

Donald T. Kramer et al., *Legal Rights of Children* (rev. 2d ed. 2005–date) [Westlaw]

Mark I. Soler et al., *Representing the Child Client* (1987–date) [Lexis]

CIVIL RIGHTS (KF1307, KF1325, KF4741–KF4786)

Michael Avery et al., *Police Misconduct: Law and Litigation* (annual) [Westlaw]

Joseph G. Cook & John L. Sobieski, *Civil Rights Actions* (1983–date) [Lexis]

Harold S. Lewis & Elizabeth J. Norman, *Civil Rights Law and Practice* (2d ed. 2004)

Michael B. Mushlin, *Rights of Prisoners* (4th ed. 2009–date) [Westlaw]

Sheldon H. Nahmod, *Civil Rights and Civil Liberties Litigation: The Law of Section 1983* (4th ed. 1997–date) [Westlaw]

Martin A. Schwartz et al., *Section 1983 Litigation* (2d–5th eds. 2003–date) [Westlaw]

Robert G. Schwemm, *Housing Discrimination: Law and Litigation* (1990–date) [Westlaw]

COMMERCIAL LAW (KF871–KF890)

Barkley Clark & Barbara Clark, *The Law of Secured Transactions under the Uniform Commercial Code* (3d ed. 2011–date) [Lexis, Westlaw]

Peter F. Coogan et al., *Secured Transactions under the
Uniform Commercial Code* (1963–date) [Lexis]

Ralph H. Folsom, *International Business Transactions*
(3d ed. 2013–date) [Westlaw]

John R. Fonseca & Patricia E. Fonseca, *Williston on
Sales* (5th ed. 1994–date)

Hawkland's Uniform Commercial Code Series
(Frederick H. Miller ed., 1982–date) [Westlaw]

Lary Lawrence et al., *Lawrence's Anderson on the
Uniform Commercial Code* (3d ed. 1981–date) [Westlaw]

James J. White & Robert S. Summers, *Uniform
Commercial Code* (6th ed. 2010–date) [Westlaw]

COMMUNICATIONS LAW (KF2761–KF2849)

Peter W. Huber et al., *Federal Telecommunications Law*
(2d ed. 1999–date)

Harvey L. Zuckman et al., *Modern Communications Law*
(1999)

CONFLICT OF LAWS (KF410–KF418)

Peter Hay et al., *Conflict of Laws* (5th ed. 2010)

Russell J. Weintraub, *Commentary on the Conflict of
Laws* (6th ed. 2010)

CONSTITUTIONAL LAW (KF4501–KF4558)

Erwin Chemerinsky, *Constitutional Law: Principles and
Policies* (5th ed. 2015)

Jennifer Friesen, *State Constitutional Law: Litigating
Individual Rights, Claims, and Defenses* (4th ed. 2006–
date)

Ronald D. Rotunda & John E. Nowak, *Treatise on Constitutional Law: Substance and Procedure* (5th ed. 2012–date) [Westlaw]

Rodney A. Smolla, *Smolla & Nimmer on Freedom of Speech* (3d ed. 1996–date) [Westlaw]

Laurence H. Tribe, *American Constitutional Law* (2d/3d eds. 1988–2000)

CONSTRUCTION LAW (KF901–KF902)

Philip L. Bruner & Patrick J. O'Connor, Jr., *Bruner & O'Connor on Construction Law* (2002–date) [Westlaw]

Construction Law (Steven G. M. Stein ed. 1986–date) [Lexis]

CONTRACTS (KF801–KF839)

Corbin on Contracts (Joseph M. Perillo ed., rev. ed. 1993–date) [Lexis]

E. Allan Farnsworth, *Farnsworth on Contracts* (3d ed. 2004–date)

Richard A. Lord, *Williston on Contracts* (4th ed. 1990–date) [Westlaw]

John Edward Murray, Jr., *Murray on Contracts* (5th ed. 2011) [Lexis]

Joseph M. Perillo, *Contracts* (7th ed. 2014)

CORPORATIONS (KF1384–KF1480, KFD213)

James D. Cox & Thomas Lee Hazen, *Cox and Hazen on Corporations* (3d ed. 2010–date) [Westlaw]

William Meade Fletcher et al., *Fletcher Cyclopedia of the Law of Private Corporations* (1931–date) [Westlaw]

Franklin A. Gevurtz, *Corporation Law* (2d ed. 2010)

Martin D. Ginsburg et al., *Mergers, Acquisitions, and Buyouts* (semiannual)

Services: *Corporate Governance Guide* (Wolters Kluwer), *Corporation Service* (Wolters Kluwer), *Mergers & Acquisitions Law Report* (BNA)

CRIMINAL LAW AND PROCEDURE
(KF9201–KF9479, KF9601–KF9763)

Randy Hertz & James S. Liebman, *Federal Habeas Corpus Practice and Procedure* (6th ed. 2011–date) [Lexis]

Thomas W. Hutchison et al., *Federal Sentencing Law and Practice* (annual) [Westlaw]

Wayne R. LaFave, *Search and Seizure: A Treatise on the Fourth Amendment* (5th ed. 2012–date) [Westlaw]

Wayne R. LaFave, *Substantive Criminal Law* (2d ed. 2003–date) [Westlaw]

Wayne R. LaFave et al., *Criminal Procedure* (3d ed. 2007–date) [Westlaw]

Paul H. Robinson, *Criminal Law Defenses* (1984–date) [Westlaw]

Charles E. Torcia, *Wharton's Criminal Law* (15th ed. 1993–date) [Westlaw]

Charles H. Whitebread & Christopher Slobogin, *Criminal Procedure* (6th ed. 2015)

Service: *Criminal Law Reporter* (BNA)

DISABILITIES (KF480, KF3469)

Peter Blanck et al., _Disability, Civil Rights Law, and Policy_ (2004)

Michael L. Perlin, _Mental Disability Law: Civil and Criminal_ (2d ed. 1998–date)

Henry H. Perritt, Jr., _Americans with Disabilities Act Handbook_ (4th ed. 2003–date)

Laura F. Rothstein & Julia Irzyk, _Disabilities and the Law_ (semiannual) [Westlaw]

DISPUTE RESOLUTION (KF3416–KF3425, KF9084–KF9086)

Sarah R. Cole et al., _Mediation: Law, Policy and Practice_ (annual) [Westlaw]

Larry E. Edmondson, _Domke on Commercial Arbitration_ (3d ed. 2003–date) [Westlaw]

Elkouri & Elkouri: How Arbitration Works (Kenneth May ed., 7th ed. 2012) [Bloomberg Law]

EDUCATION LAW (KF4101–KF4257)

Education Law (James A. Rapp ed., 1984–date) [Lexis]

William A. Kaplin & Barbara A. Lee, _The Law of Higher Education_ (5th ed. 2013)

Mark C. Weber, _Special Education Law and Litigation Treatise_ (3d ed. 2008–date)

Service: _Individuals with Disabilities Education Law Report/Special Ed Connection_ (LRP Publications)

ELDER LAW (KF390 .A4)

Lawrence A. Frolik & Melissa C. Brown, *Advising the Elderly or Disabled Client* (2d ed. 2000–date) [Westlaw]

Joan M. Krauskopf et al., *ElderLaw: Advocacy for the Aging* (2d ed. 1992–date) [Westlaw]

Social Security Law and Practice (Michael A. Rosenhouse ed., 1983–date) [Westlaw]

Services: *Medicare and Medicaid Guide* (Wolters Kluwer), *Social Security Reporter* (Wolters Kluwer)

EMPLOYMENT AND LABOR LAW (KF3301–KF3580)

The Developing Labor Law: The Boards, the Courts, and the National Labor Relations Act (John E. Higgins, Jr. ed., 6th ed. 2012–date) [Bloomberg Law]

Howard C. Eglit, *Age Discrimination* (2d ed. 1994–date)

Employment Law (Mark A. Rothstein ed., 5th ed. 2014–date) [Westlaw]

Robert A. Gorman & Matthew W. Finkin, *Basic Text on Labor Law: Unionization and Collective Bargaining* (2d ed. 2004)

Arthur Larson & Lex K. Larson, *Larson's Workers' Compensation Law* (1952–date) [Lexis]

Lex K. Larson, *Employment Discrimination* (2d ed. 1994–date) [Lexis]

Barbara Lindemann et al., *Employment Discrimination Law* (5th ed. 2012–date) [Bloomberg Law]

Henry H. Perritt, *Employee Dismissal Law and Practice* (5th ed. 2006–date)

Services: *Collective Bargaining Negotiations and Contracts* (BNA), *Employment Coordinator* (West), *Labor Law Reporter* (CCH), *Labor Relations Reporter* (BNA), *Occupational Safety & Health Reporter* (BNA)

ENERGY AND NATURAL RESOURCES
(KF1801–KF1873, KF5500–KF5510)

American Law of Mining (Cheryl Outerbridge ed., 2d ed. 1984–date) [Lexis]

George Cameron Coggins & Robert L. Glickman, *Public Natural Resources Law* (2d ed. 2007–date) [Westlaw]

Neil E. Harl, *Agricultural Law* (1980–date) [Lexis]

Eugene Kuntz, *A Treatise on the Law of Oil and Gas* (1962–date) [Lexis]

Patrick H. Martin & Bruce M. Kramer, *Williams & Meyers, Oil and Gas Law* (1959–date) [Lexis]

Nancy Saint-Paul, *Summers Oil and Gas* (3d ed. 2004–date) [Westlaw]

A. Dan Tarlock, *Law of Water Rights and Resources* (annual) [Westlaw]

Waters and Water Rights (Amy K. Kelley ed., 3d ed. 2009–date) [Lexis]

ENVIRONMENTAL LAW (KF3775–KF3816)

Frank P. Grad et al., *Treatise on Environmental Law* (1973–date) [Lexis]

Law of Environmental Protection (Sheldon M. Novick et al. eds., 1987–date) [Westlaw]

The Law of Hazardous Waste (Susan M. Cooke ed., 1987–date) [Westlaw]

William H. Rodgers, Jr., *Environmental Law* (1986–date) [Westlaw]

Services: *Environment Reporter* (BNA), *Environmental Law Reporter* (Environmental Law Institute)

EVIDENCE (KF8931–KF8969, KF9660–KF9678)

David L. Faigman et al., *Modern Scientific Evidence* (annual) [Westlaw]

Michael H. Graham, *Handbook of Federal Evidence* (7th ed. 2012–date) [Westlaw]

McCormick on Evidence (Kenneth S. Broun ed., 7th ed. 2013) [Westlaw]

Christopher B. Mueller & Laird C. Kirkpatrick, *Federal Evidence* (4th ed. 2013–date) [Westlaw]

The New Wigmore: A Treatise on Evidence (Richard D. Friedman ed., 1st–2d eds., 2002–date) [Westlaw]

Stephen A. Saltzburg et al., *Federal Rules of Evidence Manual* (11th ed. 2015–date) [Lexis]

Weinstein's Federal Evidence (Joseph M. McLaughlin et al. eds., 1997–date) [Lexis]

John Henry Wigmore et al., *Evidence in Trials at Common Law* (4th ed. 1961–date)

FAMILY LAW (KF501–KF553)

Adoption Law and Practice (Joan H. Hollinger ed., 1988–date) [Lexis]

Jeff Atkinson, *Modern Child Custody Practice* (2d ed. 2000–date) [Lexis]

Ann M. Haralambie, *Handling Child Custody, Abuse and Adoption Cases* (3d ed. 2009–date) [Westlaw]

Laura W. Morgan, *Child Support Guidelines: Interpretation and Application* (2d ed. 2013–date) [Westlaw]

Brett R. Turner, *Equitable Distribution of Property* (3d ed. 2005–date) [Westlaw]

Service: *Family Law Reporter* (BNA)

FEDERAL PRACTICE (KF8820–KF9058, KF9650)

Erwin Chemerinsky, *Federal Jurisdiction* (6th ed. 2012)

Jack H. Friedenthal, *Civil Procedure* (5th ed. 2015)

Moore's Federal Practice (Daniel R. Coquillette et al. eds., 3d ed. 1997–date) [Lexis]

William B. Rubenstein et al., *Newberg on Class Actions* (4th/5th eds. 2002–date) [Westlaw]

Stephen M. Shapiro et al., *Supreme Court Practice* (10th ed. 2013) [Bloomberg Law]

Charles Alan Wright & Mary Kay Kane, *Law of Federal Courts* (7th ed. 2011)

Charles Alan Wright et al., *Federal Practice and Procedure* (1st–4th eds. 1969–date) [Westlaw]

Service: *The United States Law Week* (BNA)

GOVERNMENT CONTRACTS (KF843–KF869.5)

John T. Boese, Civil False Claims and Qui Tam Actions (4th ed. 2011–date) [Westlaw]

John Cibinic, Jr. et al., *Administration of Government Contracts* (4th ed. 2006).

John Cibinic, Jr. et al., *Formation of Government Contracts* (4th ed. 2011).

Services: *Federal Contracts Report* (BNA), *Government Contracts Reporter* (Wolters Kluwer)

HEALTH LAW (KF3821–KF3896)

Barry R. Furrow et al., *Health Law* (3d ed. 2015)

David W. Louisell et al., *Medical Malpractice* (1960–date) [Lexis]

James T. O'Reilly, *Food and Drug Administration* (3d ed. 2007–date) [Westlaw]

Services: *Food Drug and Cosmetic Law Reporter* (Wolters Kluwer), *Health Law Reporter* (BNA)

IMMIGRATION (KF4800–KF4848)

Austin T. Fragomen, Jr. & Steven C. Bell, *Immigration Fundamentals: A Guide to Law and Practice* (4th ed. 1996–date) [Bloomberg Law]

Charles Gordon et al., *Immigration Law and Procedure* (rev. ed. 1966–date) [Lexis]

Dan Kesselbrenner & Lory D. Rosenberg, *Immigration Law and Crimes* (semiannual) [Westlaw]

INSURANCE (KF1146–KF1238)

New Appleman on Insurance Law; *Appleman on Insurance, 2d*; *Insurance Law and Practice* (Jeffrey E. Thomas ed., 1979–date) [Lexis]

Barry R. Ostrager & Thomas R. Newman, *Handbook on Insurance Coverage Disputes* (17th ed. 2015–date)

Steven Pitt et al., *Couch on Insurance 3d* (1995–date) [Westlaw]

INTELLECTUAL PROPERTY (KF2971–KF3193)

Donald S. Chisum, *Chisum on Patents* (1978–date) [Lexis]

Paul Goldstein, *Goldstein on Copyright* (3d ed. 2005–date)

J. Thomas McCarthy, *McCarthy on Trademarks and Unfair Competition* (4th ed. 1996–date) [Westlaw]

Roger M. Milgrim & Eric E. Bensen, *Milgrim on Trade Secrets* (1967–date) [Lexis]

John Gladstone Mills III et al., *Patent Law Fundamentals* (2d ed. 1980–date) [Westlaw]

R. Carl Moy, *Moy's Walker on Patents* (4th ed. 2003–date) [Westlaw]

Melville B. Nimmer & David Nimmer, *Nimmer on Copyright* (1963–date) [Lexis]

William F. Patry, *Patry on Copyright* (2006–date) [Westlaw]

Services: *Copyright Law Reporter* (Wolters Kluwer), *Trademark Law Guide* (Wolters Kluwer)

LEGAL ETHICS (KF305–KF314)

Charles Gardner Geyh et al., *Judicial Conduct and Ethics* (4th ed. 2007–date) [Lexis]

Geoffrey C. Hazard, Jr. et al., *The Law of Lawyering* (4th ed. 2015–date)

Ronald E. Mallen & Jeffrey M. Smith, *Legal Malpractice* (annual) [Westlaw]

Ronald D. Rotunda & John S. Dzienkowski, *Legal Ethics: The Lawyer's Deskbook on Professional Responsibility* (annual) [Westlaw]

Service: *ABA/BNA Lawyer's Manual on Professional Conduct* (BNA)

LOCAL GOVERNMENT (KF5300–KF5332)

John Martinez, *Local Government Law* (2d ed. 2012–date) [Westlaw]

Eugene McQuillin et al., *The Law of Municipal Corporations* (3d ed. 1949–date) [Westlaw]

Osborne M. Reynolds, *Local Government Law* (4th ed. 2015)

MILITARY LAW (KF7201–KF7695)

Francis A. Gilligan & Frederic I. Lederer, *Court-Martial Procedure* (4th ed. 2015–date) [Lexis]

Stephen A. Saltzburg et al., *Military Rules of Evidence Manual* (8th ed. 2015–date) [Lexis]

David A. Schlueter, *Military Criminal Justice: Practice and Procedure* (8th ed. 2012–date) [Lexis]

PARTNERSHIPS AND LIMITED LIABILITY COMPANIES (KF1371–KF1381)

Carter G. Bishop & Daniel S. Kleinberger, *Limited Liability Companies: Tax and Business Law* (1994–date) [Westlaw]

William A. Gregory, *The Law of Agency and Partnership* (3d ed. 2001)

Christine Hurt et al., *Bromberg and Ribstein on Partnership* (2d ed. 2014–date)

Larry E. Ribstein & Robert R. Keatinge, *Ribstein and Keatinge on Limited Liability Companies* (semiannual) [Westlaw]

PRODUCTS LIABILITY (KF1296–KF1297)

Louis R. Frumer et al., *Products Liability* (1960–date) [Lexis]

David G. Owen & Mary J. Davis, *Madden & Owen on Products Liability Law* (4th ed. 2014–date) [Westlaw]

Services: *Product Safety & Liability Reporter* (BNA), *Products Liability Reports* (Wolters Kluwer)

PROPERTY (KF560–KF720)

Grant S. Nelson et al., *Real Estate Finance Law* (6th ed. 2014) [Westlaw]

Powell on Real Property (Michael Allan Wolf ed., 1949–date) [Lexis]

Joseph William Singer, *Property* (4th ed. 2013)

William B. Stoebuck & Dale A. Whitman, *The Law of Property* (3d ed. 2000)

Thompson on Real Property (David A. Thomas ed., 2d/3d eds. 1998–date) [Lexis]

REMEDIES (KF9010–KF9039)

Dan B. Dobbs, *Dobbs Law of Remedies: Damages, Equity, Restitution* (2d ed. 1993)

George E. Palmer & Lawrence Kaplan, *The Law of Restitution* (1978–date)

Linda L. Schlueter, *Punitive Damages* (6th ed. 2010–date) [Lexis]

SECURITIES (KF1066–KF1084, KF1428–KF1457)

Harold S. Bloomenthal & Samuel Wolff, *Securities and Federal Corporate Law* (2d ed. 1998–date) [Westlaw]

Harold S. Bloomenthal & Samuel Wolff, *Securities Law Handbook* (annual) [Westlaw]

Alan R. Bromberg et al., *Bromberg & Lowenfels on Securities Fraud and Commodities Fraud* (2d ed. 1994–date) [Westlaw]

Thomas Lee Hazen, *Treatise on the Law of Securities Regulation* (6th ed. 2009–date) [Westlaw]

Donald C. Langevoort, *Insider Trading: Regulation, Enforcement, and Prevention* (1991–date) [Westlaw]

Louis Loss et al., *Securities Regulation* (4th/5th eds. 2006–date)

Services: *Blue Sky Law Reports* (Wolters Kluwer), *Federal Securities Law Reports* (Wolters Kluwer), *Securities Regulation & Law Report* (BNA)

TAXATION (KF6271–KF6645)

Boris I. Bittker & James S. Eustice, *Federal Income Taxation of Corporations and Shareholders* (7th ed. 2000–date) [Westlaw]

Boris I. Bittker & Lawrence Lokken, *Federal Taxation of Income, Estates, and Gifts* (2d/3d eds. 1989–date) [Westlaw]

Boris I. Bittker et al., *Federal Income Taxation of Individuals* (3d ed. 2002–date) [Westlaw]

Jerome R. Hellerstein & Walter Hellerstein, *State Taxation* (3d ed. 1998–date) [Westlaw]

William S. McKee et al., *Federal Taxation of Partnerships and Partners* (4th ed. 2007–date) [Westlaw]

Jacob Mertens, Jr. et al., *The Law of Federal Income Taxation* (1942–date) [Westlaw]

Michael I. Saltzman, *IRS Practice and Procedure* (2d ed. 1991–date) [Westlaw]

Richard B. Stephens et al., *Federal Estate and Gift Taxation* (9th ed. 2013–date) [Westlaw]

Arthur B. Willis & Philip F. Postlewaite, *Partnership Taxation* (7th ed. 2011–date) [Westlaw]

Services: *Federal Estate and Gift Tax Reporter* (CCH), *Federal Tax Coordinator 2d* (RIA), *Standard Federal Tax Reporter* (CCH), *State Tax Guide* (CCH), *United States Tax Reporter* (RIA)

TORTS (KF1246–KF1327)

Dan B. Dobbs et al., *The Law of Torts* (2d ed. 2011–date) [Westlaw]

Richard A. Epstein, *Torts* (1999)

Fowler V. Harper et al., *Harper, James and Gray on Torts* (3d ed. 2006–date)

J. Thomas McCarthy, *The Rights of Publicity and Privacy* (annual) [Westlaw]

Rodney A. Smolla, *Law of Defamation* (2d ed. 1999–date) [Westlaw]

Stuart M. Speiser et al., *The American Law of Torts* (1983–date)

TRUSTS AND ESTATES (KF726–KF780)

George G. Bogert et al., *The Law of Trusts and Trustees* (2d/3d eds. 1977–date) [Westlaw]

William M. McGovern et al., *Wills, Trusts and Estates* (4th ed. 2010)

Jeffrey A. Schoenblum, *Page on the Law of Wills* (1960–date) [Lexis]

Austin Wakeman Scott et al., *Scott and Ascher on Trusts* (5th eds. 2006–date)

ZONING AND LAND USE (KF5599–KF5710)

Julian Conrad Juergensmeyer & Thomas E. Roberts, *Land Use Planning and Development Regulation Law* (3d ed. 2012)

Daniel R. Mandelker, *Land Use Law* (5th ed. 2003–date) [Lexis]

Nichols on Eminent Domain (Julius L. Sackman et al. eds., 3d ed. 1964–date) [Lexis]

Arden H. Rathkopf et al., *Rathkopf's The Law of Zoning and Planning* (1975–date) [Westlaw]

Patrick J. Rohan et al., *Zoning and Land Use Controls* (1977–date) [Lexis]

Patricia E. Salkin, *American Law of Zoning* (5th ed. 2008–date) [Westlaw]

RESOURCE INDEX

References are to Pages

Note: Entries in plain type are online resources, available either for free or by subscription. Entries in italics are print publications, many of which are also available online. See the *Nutshell*'s companion website <libguides.law.virginia.edu/nutshell12> for a regularly updated collection of links to all websites mentioned in the book.

SUBJECT INDEX

References are to Pages